An Archaeological
Guide to Bahrain

An Archaeological Guide to Bahrain

Rachel MacLean and
Timothy Insoll

Archaeopress
Gordon House
276 Banbury Road
Oxford
OX2 7ED

www.archaeopress.com

An Archaeological Guide to Bahrain

ISBN 978-1-905739-36-3

Printed in England by Information Press

Rachel MacLean is a graduate of Queen's University, Belfast and gained a PhD in Archaeology from the University of Cambridge in 1996. Timothy Insoll is a graduate of Sheffield University and was awarded his PhD in Archaeology by the University of Cambridge in 1995. He is currently a Professor of Archaeology at the University of Manchester and is the author of several volumes, including *The Archaeology of Islam* (1999) and *The Land of Enki in the Islamic Era* (2005). They have both worked as archaeologists in various parts of the world and in 2001 they lived and worked on Bahrain for a year, beginning a fascination with its unique archaeological heritage that has resulted in the production of this guidebook.

Acknowledgements

This book could not have been written without the continuing support and interest of His Highness the Crown Prince, Shaikh Salman bin Hamad bin Isa Al Khalifa. His Highness helped establish the Early Islamic Bahrain Project that first brought us to Bahrain in 2001 and has continued to support our work here over the years, commissioning this guidebook so that we could share our enthusiasm with Bahrainis, residents and visitors to the country. We must also thank Mr Will Griffiths of the Crown Prince's Court for ensuring that the commissioning process and our fieldtrips to Bahrain have been organized so efficiently. Bahrain's Minister of Culture and Information, Shaikha Mai bint Mohammed Al Khalifa, has also been extremely helpful and her passion for Bahrain's Heritage is a great asset to the nation. Thanks are also due to Salman Almahari, Chief of the Heritage Preservation Department, and Abdulla Sulitiy, Head of Archaeology and Heritage.

Archaeological colleagues in Denmark provided us with access to their wonderful archives and gave us the benefit of their experience, and we must particularly thank Flemming Højlund of Aarhus University for his help and kindness. Steffen Laursen of Aarhus University kindly shared his published and unpublished work with us. Robert Killick, former director of the London-Bahrain Archaeological Expedition, gave us free access to the Expedition's image archives of their work at Saar.

Finally, thanks are due to David Davison of Archaeopress for the efficiency and speed with which the Guidebook was produced, printed and shipped, and to Karl Lunn for his splendid illustrations.

Contents

Chapter One

Introduction to Bahrain: The Archaeological Wonder of the Arabian Gulf

Today, people are drawn from all over the world to the vibrant cosmopolitan kingdom that is modern Bahrain. The unique nature of the country, its location and natural resources, the mix of rich cultural traditions and modern dynamism, and the friendliness of its citizens, all make for a country with an international reputation far greater than its geographical size would suggest. This is not only a recent phenomenon. Bahrain has played a similar role for many centuries, attracting people from elsewhere in Arabia, Asia, Africa and Europe who brought with them new ideas and ways of living, and who left their mark on the islands. This book examines the archaeological evidence left by these people to show how they lived on Bahrain. Moreover, it acts as a guide to the most important sites that can be visited today, giving directions to find them and describing what the visitor can see and understand of Bahrain's past from its archaeology.

The Geography of Bahrain

"The land is silver and the sea is pearl". Bahraini description quoted by Capt. E.L. Durand 1880.

Modern Bahrain encompasses two groups of islands, officially numbering thirty-three, which lie in the Gulf of Salwa, an arm of the Arabian Gulf (see **Fig.** 1.01). The most important group, lying only 24km from the coast of Saudi Arabia, is composed of six

Fig. 1.01
The location of Bahrain
in the Arabian Gulf.

main islands: Bahrain (or Awal), the largest in the group at 48km by 16km, Muharraq, Sitra, Nabih Salih, Jidda and Umm-an-Nasaan. These islands are joined by bridges and causeways, with most of Bahrain's population living in the north of Bahrain (Awal), Muharraq and Sitra. The second group of islands, the Hawar Islands, lie further to the south about 1.5km from the coast of Qatar and are only sparsely populated.

The sea surrounding the islands is shallow, and the land is largely flat and arid, being a mix of stony and sandy desert, semi-desert and salt flats (known as *sabkha*). The highest point on Bahrain, Jebel Dukhan, the 'Mountain of Smoke', lies in the middle of a central depression and is only 122m above sea-level. The islands are primarily characterised by a layer of hard limestone marked by occasional shallow rocky cliffs and dry wadis, and in many places covered with sand dunes.

The shallow seas in which Bahrain lies are amongst the warmest on the planet and contribute to the very high temperatures reached in the summer months (as high as 46°C in May) as the waters heat quickly resulting in high levels of humidity. In addition, the Zagros Mountains in Iran cause winds to sweep down to Bahrain collecting fine particles from the dust bowls of Iraq and Saudi Arabia. This punishing climate and the aridity of much of the islands suggest that Bahrain would prove an inhospitable environment for past settlement.

Bahrain, however, was blessed with a natural advantage. In the north of Awal underground springs emerge from the ground to form natural oases, and it is this supply of freshwater that allowed people to settle and thrive. Nabih Salih, too, was reknowned for its many freshwater springs. Throughout the centuries the natural springs were supplemented with artesian wells and canal systems (*qanats*) and Bahrain has long been famous for its lush green date plantations and gardens. Five thousand years ago the inhabitants of Bahrain worshipped Enki, the god of 'sweet waters under the earth'. Today, the blessing of this 'second sea' of freshwater is referenced in the name of the nation – *Al-Bahrayn* means in Arabic 'The Two Seas'.

Bahrain's Natural Resources

The deserts of Bahrain are a relatively impoverished environment, yet are still home to some 200 species of desert plants and to a range of wildlife. Animals such as the *dhab*, or spiny-tailed lizard, the Arabian sand gazelle, the lesser three-toed jerboa, the long-eared desert hedgehog and cape hare may still be seen in the wilder parts of the desert, and other indigenous and Arabian species are being successfully bred and protected at the Al Areen Wildlife Park. Numerous bird species are found in the various habitats of the island, desert, coast and gardens. The Hawar islands in particular are renowned for their birdlife, which at certain times of the year includes 200,000 Socotra cormorants and 1,000 flamingos.

The seas around the islands support a wealth of marine wildlife. Bahrainis exploit the shallow tidal and sub-tidal zones with hadra fish traps, large semi-permanent structures made from palm branches that funnel fish or animals into a circular trap, where they are kept alive for harvesting at low tide. Various types of sailing craft are used to fish the shallow waters (eg. the little 3m *shasha*) and the deeper waters further offshore (eg. the *shu'ai*, which can be 50m in length). In addition to a range of fish species, shrimps, sea turtles and dugong have all contributed to the local diet, and the long-standing importance of this contribution we can clearly see in the archaeological evidence.

These warm shallow seas were not just the source of food, the beds of sea-grass which flourish here are ideal breeding grounds for pearl oysters. The natural pearls of Bahrain have been famous for more than four thousand years – Mesopotamian tablets from this date refer to the "fish-eyes" or pearls from Dilmun (Bahrain). Bahrain's pearl-fishing attracted trade and brought Bahrain wealth for millennia, until, with the development of the cultured pearl industry in the Far East and the beginning of oil exploitation in Bahrain, it collapsed in the 1930s. Today, although pearl-diving is no longer a major economic activity, Bahrain remains one of the world's most important trading centres for high quality pearls.

Just as this economic crisis hit, however, the geology of the islands was to provide a new source of natural riches. In 1932 oil was struck in the centre of the island, eventually producing up to 15 million tonnes a year and bringing with it the great wealth that initiated the rapid development of Bahrain throughout the twentieth century. Today, with the supplies of oil declining, Bahrain has diversified, adapted and innovated with an economy in which banking, natural gas, aluminium smelting and ship repair all play a part. Its highly developed communication and transport facilities attract multinational firms to its shores, continuing a tradition begun when traders were first welcomed over four thousand years ago.

Bahrain – International Crossroads

Bahrain lies in a unique position. It is situated halfway between the mouth of the Tigris and Euphrates Rivers at the north-western end of the Arabian Gulf and the Strait of Hormuz at its south-eastern end (see **Fig.** 1.01) - halfway between two major waterways of the great Near Eastern civilizations and the narrow straits leading to the Indian Ocean. It lies at the crossroads of the maritime routes linking the Near East to the Indian sub-continent. This strategic position and its good harbours made Bahrain an obvious trading port, and the abundant freshwater of its springs and its luxuriant gardens made it an attractive stopover for merchants and sailors. With this combination of natural advantages Bahrain was able to exercise control over trade from a very early date. Indeed, the archaeological evidence shows that Bahrain was welcoming a cosmopolitan mix of people and goods to its islands in the Bronze Age, four and a half thousand years ago.

Bahrain has always been home to a diverse and innovative people, open to new goods and new ideas, as the archaeological sites highlighted in this book show. Bahrainis have made the most of the unique qualities of these islands, have created gardens of great beauty and abundance between the desert and the sea, and have developed a country in which strangers are welcomed without being allowed to damage the traditions and nature of the indigenous society. Despite the unprecedented scale and speed of Bahrain's current development, there still remain protected archaeological sites where we can gain a glimpse of these past communities. This book acts as a guide to a range of sites, chosen because of their accessibility for the visitor and because of the rich archaeological material they have produced (see **Fig.** 1.02). It takes the visitor to ancient temples, tombs, markets, forts, and the earliest mosque on the islands. We hope you enjoy exploring Bahrain's past as much as we have done.

A Bahrain Timeline

Earliest Occupation 5,000-4,000 BC. The first evidence for occupation on Bahrain dates from about 5,000-4,000 BC. Before this time Bahrain had been part of the Arabian mainland, indeed fifteen thousand years ago the Arabian Gulf itself did not exist, and any evidence for earlier occupation was drowned long ago by rising sea levels. The earliest sites on Bahrain, presumably of fishing communities, are found around the coast and here evidence is largely limited to stone tools, including finely carved barbed arrowheads, and sherds of painted Ubaid pottery. This pottery originated in Mesopotamia and shows that Bahrainis were already trading with the wider world at this early date.

The Early Bronze Age: Early Dilmun 2,500-1,800 BC. References to the land of Dilmun appear in Archaic Texts found at Uruk, Mesopotamia, in 3,300 BC. Bahrain was to become the centre of the kingdom of Dilmun, and we have extensive evidence from this period, the first settlements dating from

2,200 BC. An Early Dilmun city once existed at the site of Qala'at al-Bahrain, an important trading stop on the routes stretching north to Mesopotamia and Assyria, south to Oman and Africa and east to The Indus Valley. We also have evidence of ritual life, with the construction of the temple at Barbar, of village life at Saar, and of the treatment of the dead with the many prehistoric burial mounds that were first constructed during this period.

The Middle Bronze Age: Middle Dilmun 1,800-1,000 BC. In the fifteenth century BC the Kassite dynasty gained control of Babylonia, and their influence stretched as far as Bahrain. The Kassite governor's palace was based at Qala'at al-Bahrain, and the city was rebuilt with great warehouses to store its imports and exports.

The Iron Age: Late Dilmun 1,000-400 BC. By the seventh century BC Bahrain had come under Assyrian influence and the city at Qala'at al-Bahrain was rebuilt yet again. The last mention of the name of Dilmun is on a tablet dating from 544 BC.

Tylos 300 BC-AD 600. Alexander the Great, on his return from India, ordered the exploration of the Arabian side of the Gulf, and in about 325 BC a Greek expedition reached Bahrain. From this date Bahrain was known by its Greek name Tylos, a name that persisted until the second century AD, and some Hellenistic influences can be seen in the early part of this period. In AD 129 Bahrain fell under Parthian control, and then Sassanian control as the Sassanians succeeded the Parthians in Iran.

Early Islamic Bahrain AD 629-900. The message of Muhammad was brought to Bahrain by letter in the seventh year of the Hijra by al-Ala 'ibn al-Hadrami, following which many Arabs and Persians, including the Arab governor, converted to Islam. At this time Bahrain was a very cosmopolitan society which also included Jews, Christians and

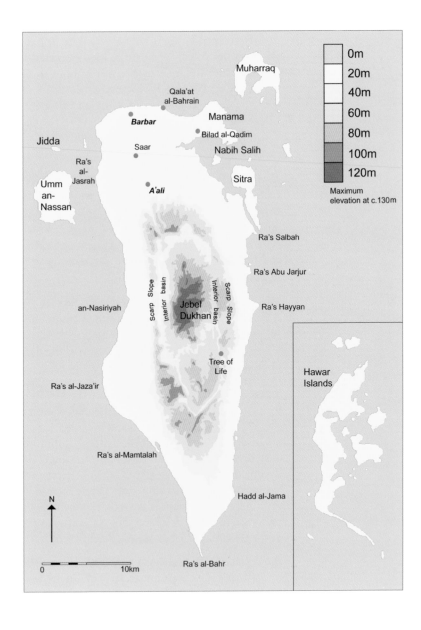

Zoroastrians, and it often acted as a refuge for political and religious fugitives. The excavations at Bilad al-Qadim give us a glimpse of this period.

Carmathians AD 900-1077. Bahrain became associated with the Carmathian state in the early tenth century. The Carmathians were a Shi'a Ismaili group centred in Eastern Arabia who revolted against the Abbasid Caliphate, attacking Hajj pilgrims and then Mecca itself in AD 930, carrying off the Black Stone from the Kaba and demanding a ransom for its return. They were finally defeated in AD 1076, and their reign in Bahrain had ceased by the following year.

Post-Carmathian Dynasties AD 1077-1520. Following the defeat of the Carmathians, Bahrain was ruled by the Uyunids until the mid-thirteenth century. At this point "greater Bahrain" was split, the island of Awal being separated from the mainland it fell under the influence of the eastern side of the Gulf, firstly the Amirs of Qays, then the Atabegs of Fars, the Salgharids and then the Princes of Hurmuz. However, by the start of the sixteenth century Bahrain was no longer paying the yearly tribute to Hurmuz.

The Portuguese, the Persians and the Omanis AD 1520-1783. During the early years of the sixteenth century Portugal had become drawn to the great wealth of Hurmuz, occupying it by force in 1507, before turning their attention to Bahrain, the pearl fisheries of Bahrain making it a particularly desirable prize. The first siege of Bahrain began in 1521, and from this date power shifted between Portuguese controlled Hurmuz and an independent Bahrain as revolt followed siege, followed revolt, followed siege. The Ottoman Turks also attempted, unsuccessfully, to wrest control of Bahrain in 1559. In 1602 the Persian empire took control of Bahrain, and was to retain it until the turn of the century when the Omanis

Fig. 1.02
The archaeological sites on Bahrain discussed in this guide.

invaded, driving most of the Bahraini population to Qatif. In 1720 the Persians purchased Bahrain from the Omanis for a considerable sum of money, only to see a second Omani invasion in 1738. The Persians regained control the following year.

The Al Khalifa AD 1783-. The Al Khalifa were members of the Bani Utbah clan, originally nomads who settled in Kuwait in 1716. They first visited Bahrain to buy pearls, but, following trouble between the Persians and the wider clan, the Al Khalifa emerged victorious to become the new rulers of Bahrain. Under their governance trade flourished and Bahrain gained control of the entire Gulf pearl trade. In 1813 Bahrain was described by J.M.Kennier as, "the finest island in the Gulf", and it has continued to grow in prosperity under Al Khalifa rule.

Chapter Two

Qala'at al-Bahrain

Bahrain's largest ancient monument, Qala'at al-Bahrain, or Bahrain Fort, is also its most extensively studied and most visited archaeological site. Many years of painstaking excavation, followed by an ambitious programme of restoration, have resulted in the atmospheric building that stands today, facing out to sea, less than 5km from the centre of Manama. It is a favourite spot with many Bahrain residents who have watched the sunset from the top of its wide, white, walls. Although the restored Portuguese fort is the most prominent feature of the site, it in fact sits on top of a large tell, a mound which has built up over many years of occupation. Excavations by Danish and French teams, in collaboration with the Bahraini Ministry of Culture and National Heritage, have revealed a history of settlement that dates back to the third millennium BC. This is the site of the ancient "Capital of Dilmun", of a substantial medieval Islamic town, and finally of the imposing sixteenth-century Portuguese fort which gives the place its name, Qala'at being Arabic for fort. It has been described as the very "memory" of Bahrain. Qala'at al-Bahrain, which is easily accessible from Manama and free to all, should not be missed by any resident or visitor to Bahrain who has an interest in the past. It is thought to be the largest archaeological site in the entire Gulf (only Thaj in Saudi Arabia being bigger according to the archaeologist Geoffrey Bibby, 1986: 108) and of such importance that it was declared a UNESCO World Heritage Site in 2005.

Fig. 2.01
Sheikh Salman visiting
the excavations in
1956. P.V. Glob is
wearing a white
Greenland anorak.
(Photo. Moesgard
Museum).

Directions to Site

Qala'at al-Bahrain is located on the north coast of
Bahrain, between the village of Karranah and the
Seef district of Manama. It is signposted from the
main Sheikh Khalifa Bin Salman Highway. The site
museum is open from Tuesdays to Sundays, 8am
to 8pm. It is closed on Mondays. The Fort itself is
open every day of the week and entry is free. Entry
to the museum costs 500 fils. The museum also has
an excellent audioguide to the site, which is free to
use. There is a very pleasant café at the site that is
open seven days a week.

Past Research

The Danish archaeologist P.V. Glob was first encouraged to travel to Bahrain by his friend and colleague Geoffrey Bibby, a British Assyriologist who had spent several years on Bahrain in the 1940s working for an oil company. Initially attracted by the spectacular burial fields, they arrived in Bahrain in 1953 with the goodwill and financial support of the then ruler, Sheikh Salman bin Hamed Al Khalifa (see **Fig.** 2.01), and quickly established a base at Qala'at al-Bahrain. Here they conducted excavations annually until 1978, discovering the remains of a 4,000 year-old city under the walls of the fort which they interpreted as the capital of the ancient land of Dilmun.

The long association of the Danish team with Bahrain continues to the present day, and their enjoyment of the island's culture contributed to the fruitfulness of their working relationship. Glob's original expedition employed specialists from the village of Beni Jamrah to build a camp of traditional *barastis* (palm-leaf houses) where they lived for three months each year (see **Fig.** 2.02). As work on the excavations progressed, two rooms in the northwest bastion of the fort were cleared of sand and used by the Danish team and their Bahraini colleagues for parties and special feasts (see **Fig.** 2.03). Oysters were gathered from the beach beside the fort and, whilst the Bahrainis drank tea, the Danes celebrated with champagne. Sheikh Salman presented all the members of the team with fine Arab robes in 1956, and Glob in particular acquired a taste for local dress. The successful collaboration between the Danes and Bahrainis culminated in the opening of the Bahrain National Museum in 1988, which was designed by Danish architects Knud Holscher.

In 1977 a French archaeological mission, led by Monik Kervran and Pierre Lombard, began

Fig. 2.02
The Danish camp at
Qala'at al-Bahrain
in the 1950s. The
traditional barasti
houses were built by
local villagers (Photo.
Moesgard Museum).

Fig. 2.03
Danes and Bahrainis
celebrate in the fort
bastion in 1959 (Photo.
Moesgard Museum).

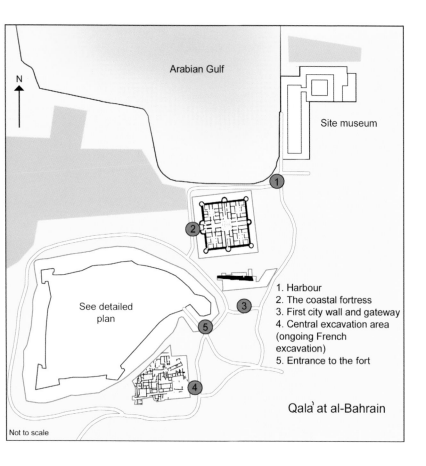

Arabian Gulf

N

Site museum

See detailed plan

1. Harbour
2. The coastal fortress
3. First city wall and gateway
4. Central excavation area (ongoing French excavation)
5. Entrance to the fort

Qala' at al-Bahrain

Not to scale

Fig. 2.04
A plan of the archaeological site of Qala'at al-Bahrain.

Fig. 2.05 (overleaf)
The buildings of the Dilmun city uncovered by the French archaeologist Pierre Lombard and his team. (Photo. Insoll and MacLean).

their own excavations at Qala'at al-Bahrain. They continued the work begun by the Danes, extending the excavations of the tell below the fort walls. Kervran led excavations of an earlier Islamic fort, uncovered by the Danes on the northern, seaward slope of the tell, which she published in 1982. Lombard's excavations of the ancient city still continue, and publication is eagerly awaited. The excellent Qala'at al-Bahrain site museum and audio-guide clearly show the great contribution of French archaeologists to the understanding of Bahrain's past, a contribution which was publicly

acknowledged in 2007, when the Government of Bahrain awarded medals to Monik Kervran and Pierre Lombard.

The Site Today

The excellent audio-guide, available free from the museum, gives a detailed description of the site. However, for those visiting when the museum is closed, or without the time for the guide, a brief description of the site today is provided here (see **Fig.** 2.04).

Thanks to the splendid programme of restoration that has been completed by the Ministry of Culture and Information, as you arrive at the site today the great fort that dominates the landscape appears much as it would have done in the sixteenth century AD. The path from the car park, however, leads you past the traces of life from much earlier times. The small bay around which you walk was once the safe harbour at the end of the channel through which the ships bringing the wealth of China, India, Arabia, Mesopotamia and Africa sailed. The remains of the medieval lighthouse, now just a low stump of masonry, can still be seen at the old mouth of the harbour.

Continuing along the path you pass in front of the medieval coastal fortress, the regular room pattern clearly visible from the walls still standing, and as you climb up the hill you will pass the main gate in the fort's western wall.

Once on the top of the tell the extent of the archaeological site becomes apparent – the entire area in front of you within the boundary wall is covered with the debris of the past four thousand years. Behind the coastal fort the wall of the very first city built on Bahrain has been left exposed, its main gateway facing the old harbour. More Dilmun period buildings can be seen to the south of the main fort (see **Fig.** 2.05) – a great view of this area can be obtained from up on the fort parapet. The French archaeological team hope to resume excavations in this area in 2010, having paused work during the UNESCO listing of the site and the construction of the museum, so lucky visitors may be able to see further work in progress.

The 'Portuguese' Fort itself has been restored to its former imposing glory, using a combination of the standing walls, the evidence from excavations and documentary evidence. Entering through the main gate you can explore the walkways, courtyards and various rooms at will, walking in the footsteps of past garrisons. Make sure to look out for military features such as gunports in the thick stone walls, and more mundane features such as the *madbasa* used for producing date syrup, and to enjoy the wonderful views from its ramparts in which old and new Bahrain can be seen side by side.

The Story from Archaeology

The Ancient Capital of Dilmun

"The land of Dilmun is blessed, the land of Dilmun is pure,

The land of Dilmun is luminous, the land of Dilmun is radiant."

(Hymn of praise to Dilmun at the beginning of the myth of "Enki and Ninhursag", quoted by André-Salvini 1999: 44.)

The land of Dilmun appears from the end of the 4th millennium BC in the myths, poems and even military inscriptions of the early Mesopotamian civilizations. It is there in the world's earliest known texts from Uruk, it is carved into the bas-reliefs on the walls of the palace of Sargon of Assyria at

Khorsabad, it appears in Nineveh and Nippur. Michael Rice has even argued that the land known to the Mesopotamians as Dilmun is described in the Pyramid Texts of Egypt, and appears in inscriptions in the Horus Temple at Edfu (1986). It appears in the Sumerian creation myth of "Enki and Ninhursag" where it is linked to the origins of the world and blessed by the gods with abundant pure, fresh water. Whilst Sumer is seen as the centre of the civilized world, Dilmun functions as an international marketplace, a great trading crossroads through which exotic goods were funnelled to Sumer.

In 1880 the French linguist Jules Oppert, best known for his work with Henry Rawlinson on the decipherment of the ancient Assyrian language cuneiform, suggested in an article published in the *Journal Asiatique* that Dilmun was in fact the island of Bahrain. The first archaeological support for his theory was provided the same year by a black basalt stone discovered by a British officer, Captain Edward Durand, in a mosque in Bilad al Qadim. On it was a cuneiform inscription which proclaimed, in Babylonian, that one Rimum was a humble servant of the god Enzak, protector of Dilmun. Following a study of the inscription, Henry Rawlinson announced that Bahrain had indeed once been the fabled land of Dilmun. Further archaeological evidence emerged slowly, as very little work was done on Bahrain before the Danish expedition of 1953, despite growing interest in the exploration of ancient Dilmun. Indeed, in 1912 the famous archaeologist Flinders Petrie, "Father of Modern Egyptology", had urged a young T.E Lawrence ('Lawrence of Arabia') to undertake digs in Bahrain. Lawrence declined; he had a very different role to play in Arabia. The vast burial fields of Bahrain were the initial attraction for Glob and Bibby, but the huge tell at Qala'at al-Bahrain and the realisation that it represented many centuries of settlement led to their discovery of a site they identified as the "Capital of Dilmun" (see **Fig.** 2.06).

Early Dilmun

The earliest occupation at Qala'at al-Bahrain dates from c. 2,200 BC and was found on the northern side of the tell, close to the sea. It is the only known settlement of this date in all of eastern Arabia (Højlund 1999). The Danes discovered complexes of small stone-walled, multi-roomed houses with plaster floors. Their occupants had a fully developed oasis agriculture, cultivating date palms and cereals, herding cattle, sheep and goats. Analysis of animal bones found in the excavations shows that cattle were used as draught animals and provided most of the meat in the diet, sheep were kept for wool and meat, and goats were kept mainly for milk. Fishing contributed a significant part of the diet, with the occasional addition of turtle, cormorant, dolphin and dugong.

Copper played an important role in their economy. Many fragments of copper tools were found, including a complete fishhook, and the discovery of a large copper-casting workshop containing a number of various sized crucibles used for smelting the copper and numerous open moulds shows that this was already a specialised profession. Interestingly, in the Mesopotamian records the name of Dilmun is often associated with copper objects. No copper deposits exist in Bahrain, but at this period copper mining was becoming an important economic activity in the land of Magan (the Oman peninsula). Copper from one of the crucibles at Qala'at al-Bahrain has been analysed and was found to be compatible with copper from the Oman peninsula (Højlund 1999: 74), suggesting that the community on Bahrain were involved in the importing of copper, which they processed before exporting to the cities of Mesopotamia.

Fig. 2.06 (overleaf) A reconstruction of the Early Dilmun city, by the Danish artist Thorkil Ebert. Ships carrying exotic items from distant lands arrive to trade with these early Bahrainis, entering the city through the great gates. (Image Moesgard Museum).

This small settlement at Qala'at al-Bahrain was already acting as a trading hub. It has been suggested that the ancient channel which runs from the sea to the shore beside the site may even date from this Early Dilmun period, though as yet this has not been proven. Ships were, however, landing with cargos of exotic and valuable commodities from more distant lands, destined eventually for Sumer and the cities of Mesopotamia, even travelling as far as Ebla in Syria, where we have records of the Dilmun scheckel, a unit of weight. Examples of Dilmun, Mesopotamian and Indus weights found at the site and dating from about 2,000 BC can be seen in the museum. The high status products of Sumer, such as ceramics, silver and wool, were being brought back to Bahrain by the Dilmun merchants for onward distribution. Many pieces of Mesopotamian ceramics have been found in the excavations at Qala'at al-Bahrain. From a Mesopotamian source we learn that "when the Dilmun merchants landed safely at Ur in Mesopotamia, they offered in gratitude a share of the cargo to the goddess Ningal" (quoted in Vine 1993: 48). One tablet lists such offerings as: "...copper ingots of 4 talents, 4 copper ingots of 3 talents each [360 kg], 11 scheckels of oblong pieces of bronze [91 g], 3 kidney shaped beads of cornelian, 3 fish-eyes [pearls], 8 (...) stones, 9 sila of white coral [7 lt], 3 (...) stones, $5^1/_2$ menas of rods of ivory [2.75 kg], 30 pieces of tortoiseshell (?), 1 wooden rod with copper (...), 1 ivory comb, 1 mina of copper in lieu of ivory [0.5 kg], 3 minas of elligu stone". Other tablets list items such as lapis lazuli, gold, firestone and antimony (used for eye-paint). Of these various commodities, only pearls, coral and tortoiseshell were local to Bahrain. Other items were being brought in from places such as Magan, Meluhha (possibly India or the Indus valley), and from Ethiopia and east Africa.

By the end of the third millennium BC this settlement had grown into a city and great walls had been built around it. The walls, which run at right angles, were originally 2.3 m thick, though they were later reinforced, and enclosed an area of about 15 ha. In places the wall survives to its original height, 4.3 m to the top of the parapet. The north wall has been most intensively excavated and here a small gate was found, 1.25 m in width, wide enough to allow a donkey or camel, but not a cart, to enter. The general population continued to live in small stone-walled houses, which were built right up to the north wall.

At the centre of the city, however, was a complex of monumental buildings that were laid out on either side of a plastered street 12 m in width. Three of these buildings were uncovered in the Danish excavations and appeared to have an identical floor plan, though only one building was excavated in its entirety. The walls of this building were 1.1 m thick and at least 4.5 m high. Inside, eight rooms were arranged on either side of a wide central passage, or hall, and the walls and floors were plastered. Outside the walls were of dressed stone. The scale of building has been described as "magnificent, of a magnitude and lavishness not to be surpassed in Bahrain or anywhere in the Gulf till the Islamic period" (Højlund 1999: 75). The original purpose of these magnificent buildings is not known. Excavations produced none of the debris generally associated with a domestic building (bones, charcoal, etc), the finds were few and were mainly potsherds. There was none of the more elaborate material normally associated with a luxurious dwelling. This has led to the suggestion that these three buildings were in fact used as warehouses, and were part of a much larger palace complex; to the north of the warehouses the street leads to a huge gate that may have led to other parts of this palace.

The scale of the external wall and of the great warehouses built in a prominent location in the centre of the city are evidence that this was now a significant community with a highly developed level of social and economic organization. Many people working long hours must have contributed to these public building projects. An overall plan and centralised authority are evident in the regularity of the scheme. Højlund suggests that we are seeing the economic centre of the Dilmun king's realm (Højlund 1999: 75), the very heart of Dilmun. The original narrow gate in the city wall, built for people and donkeys, had been replaced with an entrance twice as wide, with pivot stones made from a fine-grained imported black stone and sockets designed to hold a double-leafed gate (see **Fig.** 2.06). A recreation of the gate pivot can be seen in the museum. The gates faced the foreshore and the sea from which the riches of Asia, Arabia and Africa flowed into and out of Bahrain, and through them came the sailors and merchants of many lands who stopped to drink the fresh waters of the island and taste its famous dates. In the buildings just inside the gates the Danes found a large number of stamp-seals and weights (both local and imported), which led Geoffrey Bibby to suggest these were municipal offices, a customs house and port authority which controlled the merchants and their trade, and though recent interpretations have been more cautious there must have been some such control.

Middle Dilmun

The city flourished for several hundred years until, sometime after 1800 BC, circumstances changed. The great Indus Valley civilization disappeared, southern Mesopotamia withdrew economically and new trading centres arose to compete with Dilmun. The name of Dilmun vanishes from the Mesopotamian records for two centuries, and when it reappears Bahrain is now part of the Kassite

Fig. 2.07
One of the cuneiform records found in the warehouse. It details the delivery of items, including dates, honey and oil, to two local temples. (Photo. Moesgard Museum).

kingdom – the Kassite dynasty having taken control of Babylonia. A major building programme was initiated in the city at Qala'at al-Bahrain, restoring and extending the monumental buildings in the centre of the site. Kassite cuneiform tablets dating from 1,361-1,333 BC tell of the restoration of the palace sanctuary. These tablets, the southernmost ever found, can be seen in the museum.

Sometime in the early 14th century BC one of the great warehouses was destroyed by a terrible fire. Fortunately for archaeologists, remains of the goods once stored in the warehouse were preserved in the charred debris: in one room date stones, once a heap of dates; in another a pile of haematite and ochre, used for red pigments; in others large storage vessels and imported bowls and goblets. In one room was even found a collection of administrative documents in the form of cuneiform tablets and cylinder-seal impressions (see **Fig.** 2.07). To the north of these buildings was

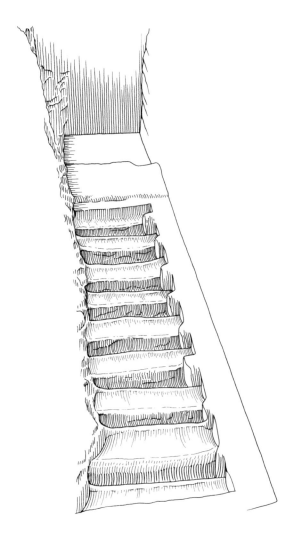

Fig. 2.08 a and b
The oldest *madbasa* found at the site, dating from the Middle Dilmun period. Used to produce date syrup, it shows that dates were already an important commodity on Bahrain over three thousand years ago. (Photo. Moesgard Museum).

also found a *madbasa* (see **Fig.** 2.08), a structure where dates were processed on a corrugated floor to produce date syrup, the earliest *madbasa* yet found and clear evidence of the quantities of dates being produced. Following the fire, all the warehouses were abandoned and left open to the elements, and the city declined for a second time.

Late Dilmun

In the monumental palace at Khorsabad, in the heart of Assyria, in bas-reliefs carved on the walls in c. 709 BC, we find the description of gifts of tribute from Uperi, "King of Dilmun". These gifts were a prudent attempt by a small and wealthy autonomous kingdom to establish favourable relations with the new ruler of a powerful and imperialist neighbour. Nevertheless, by the middle of the 7th century BC Bahrain was listed officially as an Assyrian province and in 544 BC we have a record confirming that Bahrain was under the authority of a resident administrator.

Around the 7th century BC a new complex of monumental buildings, resembling luxury residences found in Babylon, Persia and Assyria, was built at Qala'at al-Bahrain, reusing some of the older architecture and building materials, with a second major phase of construction c. 400 BC. This last building is clearly divided into smaller complexes of rooms, each complex having one main entrance and a lavatory at its far end. The lavatories contain two, occasionally three, toilets, with shield-shaped holes above subterranean plastered tanks, and are connected to drains that run under the floors (see **Fig.** 2.09). Stone lids to cover the toilets have been found. The complicated system of sanitation and drainage in the city also includes vertical drainpipes in the walls to carry rainwater to the drains that run under buildings and streets.

One of the most interesting discoveries made in this later building were about 50 snake sacrifices that were found buried beneath the floors in two of the rooms. Many of the snakes had been placed in small pottery bowls (see **Fig.** 2.10), though some were simply placed in small pits. The detailed impression of a wooden lid was found preserved in the plaster floor above one of these snake burials, even showing

Fig. 2.09
Toilets in one of the rooms of the Late Dilmun palace. The people who lived here had high standards of hygiene. (Photo. Moesgard Museum).

a crack in the original wood (F. Højlund pers comm.). The snakes have been identified as rat snakes (*Hierophis ventromaculatus*) and sea snakes (*Hydrophis lapemoides*). The rat snake is generally harmless, being non-venomous, though it can bite if it feels threatened. The sea snake, however, is very venomous. Small carnelian beads were found with half of the snakes, usually only 1-3 beads, and, less commonly, faience beads and pearls. There was also evidence of textiles in many of the burials, which have been interpreted as cloth bags in which the snakes were kept. As there was no evidence

Fig. 2.10
A sea snake buried
in a pot in the floor
of a room in the Late
Dilmun palace. The
snake was originally
1.5m long. (Photo.
Moesgard Museum).

of any injuries on the snake skeletons it has been
suggested that they may have been buried alive.
These snake burials have no parallel elsewhere and
their meaning can only be guessed, though some
religious function is the most likely explanation. It
has been suggested that for the Dilmun community
the snake may have been associated with fertility. In
the museum there is an excellent recreation of the
snake burials as they were found by archaeologists,
and a video showing their excavation.

A further curious discovery was a large number
of fragments of terracotta figurines. About two
hundred of these were found spread throughout
the excavation in later dump deposits, and consisted

mainly of fragmented male figures, many of them seated upon horses or donkeys. Again, we can only guess the meaning of these objects, which can be viewed in the museum.

The discovery of a copper workshop, with ashy copper-filled deposits, crucibles and two pot-bellows installations, indicates that copper was still playing an important role in this period. The workshop is recreated in the museum. Assyrian cuneiform texts from the late 7th century BC describe bronze tools as characteristic of the Dilmunites – elsewhere in the Middle East iron had replaced bronze. Iron was known in Bahrain: iron nails, a spearhead and a dagger, and smithing slag from the working of iron, were all found at Qala'at al-Bahrain. Below a lavatory in the palace, a pot containing a hoard of silver originally wrapped in cloth and sealed with

Fig. 2.11
The silver hoard, originally sealed inside the pot and buried beneath the floor of a lavatory. (Photo. Moesgard Museum).

Fig. 2.12
This bathtub coffin contained the burial of an adult man. He was accompanied by a rich assortment of grave goods, including a glazed vase at his feet, a stamp seal hung around his neck, an iron dagger worn on a belt around his waist, spearhead stuck into the floor and a collection of copper and bronze vessels in front of him. (Photo. Moesgard Museum).

the image of a bull below a crescent moon and star was found (see **Fig.** 2.11). The silver was mainly cut or broken fragments, which were commonly used as a medium of exchange in the region at this date.

In the final Dilmun years the dead and the living became neighbours at Qala'at al-Bahrain. In contrast to the great burial fields of Aali, discussed later in the book, burials of children in earthenware jars and of adults in pit graves or "bathtub-sarcophagi" were found under the floors of houses (see **Fig.** 2.12). A reconstruction of a burial can be seen in the museum. This is a practice that was common

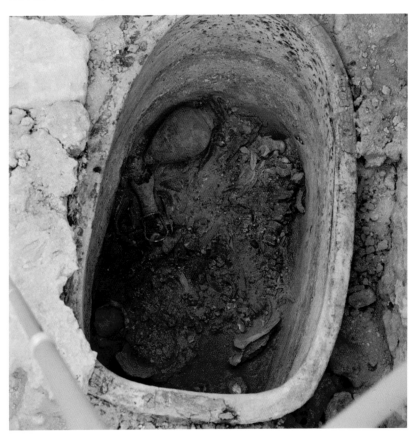

Fig. 2.13
A decorated ceramic incense burner from the Late Dilmun city. This example is similar to the incense burners used in Mesopotamia. (Photo. Moesgard Museum).

in Mesopotamia and has led to the suggestion that a Babylonian community were living amicably alongside their Bahraini neighbours. The scale and sophisticated plumbing arrangements of the later buildings and the quality and diversity of the material recovered from them (see **Fig.** 2.13) shows that Bahrain was, by the fourth century BC, once again a wealthy and relatively cosmopolitan society.

The Coastal Fort and Medieval Islamic Settlement

Whilst the main Danish excavations had been sunk in the centre of the tell, Geoffrey Bibby began his work by digging into the northern edge of the mound. Here the mound ran right down to the beach and winter storms had already exposed a section of very fine curved masonry, which Bibby believed may be a part of the wall of the city discovered by P.V. Glob (Bibby 1996: 69-70). This curved wall was in fact found to be part of a semi-circular turret jutting out from a fortification wall 3m high and nearly 2m thick, and firmly built on bedrock. Behind this wall was a street, with the remains of stone house walls on either side, which ran due south to a paved square with a central drain. From the other three sides of the square ran similar streets, lined with similar rooms, and cut at the far southern end by another fortification wall and semi-circular turret. Bibby realised that, rather than a section of well-planned town, he had found a small fort. Excavations at the four corners of the outside wall confirmed his hypothesis when he found four defensive round turrets. The discovery of a number of Chinese copper coins and a wealth of decorated glazed pottery enabled the fort to be firmly dated to the Middle Islamic period, no more than 1,000 years old. Eager to work on the older levels of the tell, Bibby moved his team south of the fort after two seasons.

In 1977 Monik Kervran and a French team continued the work begun by the Danes, uncovering a much greater part of the structure. The fort, as Bibby had thought, was indeed generally symmetrical in plan. Not only were there the four corner towers, but also semi-circular towers in the middle of three walls, whilst in the west wall two quarter-towers framed the main gate. The four internal passages ran from the central square to the outer wall. However, the four quarters divided by these passages were not identical, each bearing a different arrangement of rooms. The purpose of these various rooms was often unclear, though Kervran concluded that a number had a defensive role (1982: 65). One room, however, was clearly a *madbasa*.

The defensive nature of the building was obvious. The thickness of the walls – 2.4m – in which the only windows were loopholes or arrow-slits, and the two narrow gateways, one of which, in the northern tower, Kervran suggested could be hidden and serve as a secret passageway, clearly support Bibby's original interpretation. A later phase of French excavations discovered a moat 7m in width and reinforced with revetment walls, which had been built to protect the fort. In addition, access to the four corner towers differed, a defence strategy that, claims Kervran, may have been learned from Byzantine military architecture (1982: 70). Furthermore, in a room in the northeast corner a heap of several hundred stones, some coated with a blackish residue, were found. Kervran interpreted these as missiles waiting to be thrown at potential attackers, the residue being the remains of a naptha coating which was lit to turn the stones into flaming missiles (1982: 73).

The French excavations recovered a large number of coins (70 after the first two seasons), both Islamic and Chinese. Most of these coins were found on the floor of the tower near the south gate. Chinese coins continued in circulation for a very long time and so are of little use for dating purposes, but this was not the case with the Islamic coins, eight of which were identified as belonging to the Salgharide Atabegs of Fars (Turkish rulers) and dated to AD 1148-1280 (Negre 1982: 90). Bahrain had been conquered by Atabeg Abu Bakr Ibn Sa'd in AD 1234. Thousands of pot sherds, mainly Islamic but with about 100 Chinese sherds, were also recovered from the excavations and provided further dating evidence. They showed that Bahrain was importing Chinese ceramics from the 12th century until possibly as late as the 16th (Pirazzoli-t'Sertsevens 1982). Using this evidence, in conjunction with the style of architecture and the sites stratigraphy, Monik Kervran initially dated the construction and use of the fort to between the 10th and 13th centuries AD, suggesting that the period of Carmathian rule in the 10th and 11th centuries provides the most likely historical setting (Kervran 1982: 81).

More recently, Kervran has argued that the Islamic fort was a continuation and rebuilding of an earlier pre-Islamic fortress, and that it actually dates from around 350 AD. She has placed this earlier building within the Tylos period, when Bahrain is thought to have become part of the great area then under Greek influence. There is some dispute about this phase of the fort's life as there is as yet little to support Kervran's claims, certainly more recent work by a Danish team has found no convincing evidence for a Tylos period building.

There is, however, some evidence for a cosmopolitan community on Bahrain in the centuries around the beginning of the first millennium AD. There are a number of foreign coins: most notably 310 silver tetradrachms, Arabian copies of Alexander the Great's coinage bearing an image of Shams/Shamash an Eastern Arabian deity on the reverse which have been dated to the second century BC, and 2 copper sesterces from Rome originally minted between AD 225 and 244. In addition official documents written in Aramaic, objects from Yemen bearing South Arabian scripts and several short inscriptions in Greek have been found.

The fort had not been built in isolation. The debris from the medieval Islamic communities still lies scattered across the tell, and the visitor to Qala'at al-Bahrain today may be walking on pieces of their pots or glass fragments from their cosmetic bottles. Whilst working on other parts of the tell, the Danish teams discovered extensive evidence for medieval Islamic settlement. To the south of the fort, the remains of houses were found on both sides of the prehistoric city wall, often incorporating the wall in their structure. A large number of red-walled bread ovens, or *tannur*, were found in this area, although they invariably crumbled upon discovery.

To the southwest, massive walls had been built on top of the prehistoric wall, following their line.

Within the old city walls, on top of the prehistoric city, at least two layers of a medieval Islamic town had been built, with stone-walled houses and two further *madbasa*. Again there were several of the round clay bread ovens, together with pits and the debris from craft activities such as glass-making, ivory-carving, and in one room a number of large oyster shells were discovered alongside large jars and hammer stones suggesting some form of oyster processing (Frifelt 2001: 36, 54, 52). The whole area must have been full of bustle and activity. Part of a market, or *suq*, was identified, with rows of small shops lining an alley, its surface a well-trampled mix of clay and gypsum. The many Islamic coins that were found scattered nearby are perhaps the remnants of many small purchases and bigger business transactions. There is even a possibility that a larger building at the end of the alley built around a well may have been a *hammam*, or public bath.

To the east of the *suq* was an area the Danes named the "Merchant Quarter". Here they found more substantial houses with plastered walls and floors, and yet more *madbasa*. Expensive imported pottery, an agate pearl weight, coins, a bronze belt slider and, most spectacularly, a collection of more than 250 beads and pendants, all indicated the wealth of the occupants of these buildings. The beads and pendants were made mainly from semi-precious stones such as agate, carnelian, amethyst, and also from glass, coral and shell (Frifelt 2001: 59-60), and were found in a cache together with raw materials and tools, including a polishing stone, a small flint awl (used for piercing materials such as leather), and a collection of weights made from haematite. This collection was found outside one of the houses, possibly hidden in a small pit, and suggests the valuable stock and tools of a jeweller, which may either have been routinely hidden to prevent theft or hurriedly in response to a sudden threat. The fort, after all, had been built to defend this area from someone.

The 'Portuguese' Fort

Today, the site of Qala'at al-Bahrain is dominated by the imposing walls of the 'Portuguese' Fort. Thanks to an extensive programme of renovation and reconstruction visitors can once again walk along its ramparts and gaze out to sea, in the footsteps of soldiers from the long-gone garrisons. The natural advantages of this site are more obvious from the top of these walls: it was the highest point on the coast and controlled access to a channel deep enough for ships to sail between the shore and the sea and wide enough to be a safe mooring during bad weather. This harbour is described in the Portuguese chronicles of the 16th century. At the mouth of the channel, which lies directly north of the fort, the remains of a tower can still be seen, a base of stone 9m by 9m, which must once have controlled ships' access. From the channel itself a large number of 14th and 16th century pottery fragments have been recovered.

As we have seen, these advantages had long been recognised and a fort had been built at Qalat al-Bahrain possibly as early as the 10th century. By the 14th century, however, this had been abandoned, left to the encroaching sea and partially covered by a cemetery. Sometime after this date the new, and far more formidable, fortress was built. Excavations, conducted jointly by French and Bahraini teams, have identified three phases of construction at the fort, though the final phase destroyed much of the earlier evidence and the demands of restoration meant that complete excavation was not possible. The strategic position of Bahrain, its vital role in the trade networks which spread between India, China, Africa, the Near and Middle East, and now, at this date, Europe, its fresh water and safe harbours, made it a highly desirable territory. Throughout this period various foreign powers attempted to take control of the island and its wealth, and in defence against these hostile invasions the fort at Qala'at al-Bahrain eventually became the formidable structure that dominates the shoreline today.

Little can be said about the earliest building beyond its basic design; it was five-sided, with round towers defending its more vulnerable south and west-facing walls. On the seaward wall was a square projecting feature (a *salient*) and it is presumed that the gate opened in the east wall and was protected by an irregular *salient*. There is some evidence for narrow loop-holes in the walls, through which archers would have aimed their crossbows. It is thought that this fort must have been deserted and badly ruined by the beginning of the 16th century, as it was not used when Bahrain was besieged in AD 1521 by a joint force from Portugal and the kingdom of Hurmuz (in what is now Iran) instigated by the new governor of India, Diogo Lopes de Sequeira. Following their defeat, the Bahrainis were forced to pay tribute and were placed under the control of Portuguese agents. Within only four months, however, the Hurmuzi and Bahrainis had revolted, killing all the employees of the Portuguese factory, and freeing themselves of Portuguese control. The Portuguese regained control in AD 1523.

In AD 1529 Bahrain again revolted against Portuguese financial demands, and 800 men under the command of Badr al-Din were besieged in the fort. Therefore, we know that at sometime between 1523 and 1529 the second phase of building had been completed. In the second phase of the fort the original building was extended to the east with an enclosed triangular area (a *ravelin*), and with a low rampart around the other three sides (*fausse-braies*). The *ravelin* provided an area from which heavy artillery could cover the approach to the gate.

The whole fort was now surrounded by a moat, and the support for a drawbridge has been found on the outer edge of the ditch opposite the gate. The walls of the original fort were rebuilt and strengthened, and were now 3.3m wide in the south front.

During the 1529 siege the Portuguese used cannons to smash several holes in the walls of the fortress until, running short of powder, these became useless. The defenders, safe within their fortifications, successfully resisted the siege. A good description of the fort appears in the official Portuguese chronicle of the siege by Joao de Barros, who adds the information that, "there were some houses of poor people within the wall, and Rais Barbadin [Badr al-Din] ordered them demolished and burned before Simao de Cunha [the Portuguese commander] came" (Kervran 1988: 51). There is also a drawing of the fort made by a Portuguese during a visit to the Gulf in 1538. In the earliest known picture of the island the fort is shown flying the triangular flag of Bahrain with its Islamic crescent and the square Portuguese flag with its cross above crenellated walls, symbolizing the alliance between the Governor of Bahrain and the Kingdom of Hurmuz (represented by the Portuguese). Several vessels are shown moored at the mouth of the channel.

The great structure of Qala'at al-Bahrain that stands today is a restoration of the final phase of building (see **Fig.** 2.14). In AD 1559 the governor of Bahrain, Murad, had been besieged with 400 men inside the fortress by 1200 Turkish troops. They managed to withstand the Turks for several months before a joint Hurmuzi and Portuguese force came to Murad's aid. Following their victory a Portuguese architect, Inofre de Carvalho, who had arrived in Bahrain to build war machines to shell the Turks, devised a plan for the restoration of the fort and work began on the final phase in AD 1561. This

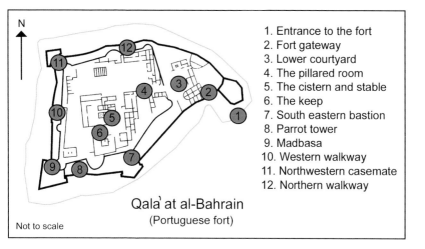

N

1. Entrance to the fort
2. Fort gateway
3. Lower courtyard
4. The pillared room
5. The cistern and stable
6. The keep
7. South eastern bastion
8. Parrot tower
9. Madbasa
10. Western walkway
11. Northwestern casemate
12. Northern walkway

Qala᾿ at al-Bahrain
(Portuguese fort)

Not to scale

Fig. 2.14
A plan of the final
phase of Qala'at al-
Bahrain – the building
which has been
restored today.

was no small undertaking. A stone on the island of
Jidda still bears the inscription, "During the month
of sha'ban of the year 968 [April-May 1561] ended
the cutting of 1100 stones for the restoration of the
tower of the fortress of Bahrain".

The Portuguese added new defences to the
older structure. Three bastions were built on the
northwest, southwest and southeast corners, and
from them artillery fire was able to cover all the
more vulnerable areas to the north, west and south.
The bastions can be explored today and their
architectural and defensive features admired; the
thickness of the walls, the domed roofs, a barrel
vault in the south-west bastion, the gunports and
the vents to allow gun-smoke to escape. In the
south bastion at the intermediate landing level a
madbasa (date-press) can be found (see **Fig.** 2.15).
In the centre of the south wall a uniquely shaped
spur tower was added to protect this particularly
vulnerable point – low down a triangular beak to
deflect bullets juts out, at the top a curved horse-
shoe allows for covering fire in all directions. In the
spur tower were the remains of a timber balcony and
a 0.5m wide gunport, most probably for a wheeled

Fig. 2.15 (overleaf)
The *madbasa* which
can be seen today in
the southern bastion
of Qala'at al-Bahrain.

cannon. The *fausse-braie*, the surrounding rampart, was raised by 1.5 – 2m, and three strong gates linked it with the inner fortress enabling the defenders to close off areas from any invaders who breached the outer defences. The unified plan of the fort and the use of modern defences implies that the architect, Inofre de Carvalho, not only supervised the building throughout, but was also well acquainted with recent architectural innovations. The bastions at Qala'at al-Bahrain were built only 25 years after they were first employed by the Italians in response to developments in artillery.

The Portuguese, however, were never able to make the best use of such a splendid building. Their ships, being far deeper in the water than the local Bahraini vessels, were never able to enter the channel and safe harbour near the fort. Instead, they were forced to moor a couple of kilometres offshore and use small boats to ferry people and goods between the two. A. Pinto da Fonseca, writing in 1601 from the King of Spain and Portugal to the Viceroy of India, complains that, "The fort is totally useless because it...is surrounded by reefs which make it impossible for ships to land there...[It] is nothing but an amoury". (Kervran 1988: 74). In 1602 the Portuguese were to lose control of Qala'at al-Bahrain, and of Bahrain. They never returned.

Though the fort was built as a defensive military structure, we should never forget that throughout its life it was home to the men who walked the ramparts. They may have been soldiers, but they also had a life beyond the various battles and sieges and were part of a wider local community. Bahraini excavations within the fort itself have recovered a range of objects that tell us of their lives: musical instruments, items of jewellery such as rings, bracelets and beads, glass vessels from Spain and Italy and ceramics from China and Iran. These objects can all be seen in the museum at the fort.

In 2009 the Ministry of Culture and Information brought in two underwater archaeologists, Eric Staples and Luca Belfioretti, to investigate the channel and harbour. They found large quantities of Islamic pottery on the seabed around the old foundations of the lighthouse at the mouth of the channel. Moreover, they concluded that the colour of the seabed in this area had been changed by the decaying of many shipwrecks over the years. This marine area, vital access to the trade and wealth which flowed in and out of the Dilmun warehouses, the Islamic town and the Portuguese fort, may prove to be one of the most important in the Gulf for old shipwrecks. The Ministry of Culture and Information is already planning further investigation.

Chapter Three

Barbar Temple

Barbar temple is the largest temple yet discovered in Bahrain and without parallel in the region. It had lain hidden beneath the sands for almost four thousand years before the Danish archaeologist P.V. Glob uncovered it in 1954. Until this discovery there was little evidence for any settlement on the island contemporaneous with the many thousands of grave-mounds that then covered Bahrain. Ernest Mackay, following his visit to the islands in 1925 suggested that they were not the tombs of Bahrainis, as "it is probable that there was not a large enough population in ancient days to account for the enormous number of tumuli on the island... we must conclude that the people who were buried on Bahrein were brought from some part of the mainland" (Rice 1984: 158). The idea of Bahrain as an 'Ancient Island of the Dead' was only overturned when the discovery of Barbar Temple, and soon after the Dilmun city at Qala'at al-Bahrain, proved that those who lay in the tombs had once lived and worshipped here.

Rather than a single temple, Barbar is, in fact, a series of temple buildings that were used and rebuilt over a number of centuries. Today, although the walls do not survive to any great height, the visitor to the site can walk around the outside of the complex and gain a good impression of its past glory. The temple was built around a freshwater spring, the centre of a water cult. It has been suggested that this pool was a temple-apsû, an entry to the subterranean freshwater ocean that was the home of Enki, the Mesopotamian god of wisdom and sweet waters. Visiting the site today, the visitor can still gaze down into the well chamber, and, looking into the home of Enki, gaze back into the Bahraini past.

Directions to Site

Barbar temple is located between the villages of Barbar and Jannusan and is signposted from the Budaiya Highway. Entry to the site is free.

Past Research

The Barbar temple tell was one of a string of mounds which ran parallel to the north coast, about one and a half kilometres inland. These mounds were described by Capt. Durand in 1880, who called them "a line of high sand-hills, chained together" (Rice 1984: 21). He recognised their probable archaeological importance, reporting the presence of a large worked stone, with "one square-cut hole, as if for the jamb of a large door...also two channels square-cut on the same face", and later regretted his lack of further investigation. Ernest Mackay, working in the 1920s, also recorded the sand-hills as grave-mounds, and though he too left them untouched, a British Political Agent did dig into one.

It was only during the first Danish archaeological survey of Bahrain in 1954 that P.V. Glob realised the significance of the temple tell. The string of mounds had been revisited by the Danish team, who confirmed the earlier identification of them as grave-mounds and, whilst noting that the Barbar mound was different, being larger in area and smaller in height, would have assumed that it too was a burial mound. P.V. Glob, however, noticed the corners of two large blocks of limestone protruding from the northern side of the tell. One of the blocks had "two square depressions cut in the top" (Bibby 1996: 49), and is possibly that previously described by Durand in 1880. Glob had two workmen quickly clear the

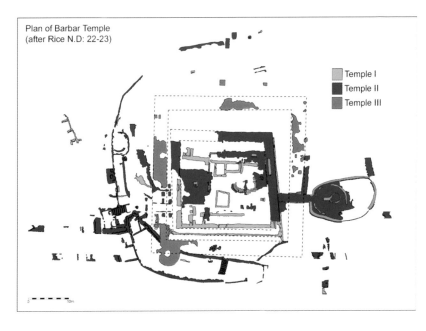

Plan of Barbar Temple
(after Rice N.D: 22-23)

Temple I
Temple II
Temple III

Fig. 3.01
Plan showing the
three phases of Barbar
Temple.

sand from these blocks and discovered they were two large cubes of stone, 1.3m across and weighing over three tons, stood upon limestone paving slabs. After this discovery, the Danes concentrated their main effort on the excavations at Barbar, digging a 2m wide trench across the mound. For a while, the hill did appear to be a new type of grave mound as the limestone paving was covered with a 3m thick layer of deliberately compacted sand, reinforced with thin layers of gypsum cement – a technique they had seen used in the construction of grave mounds. However, after opening up a larger area, 10yds (9.1m) square, around the circular structure in the centre of the mound, they found themselves looking down into the inner court of a temple in which stood a stone altar before the supports of a bench – a scene they recognised from many Mesopotamian cylinder seals. Largely under the direction of Hellmuth Andersen and Peder Mortensen, excavations continued at the site until 1961, revealing three main phases of building (see

Fig. 3.01), which were then covered for the site's protection. In 1983 the Bahrain Department of Antiquities and Museums re-excavated the site, clearing the backfill left by the Danes, to allow this very important site to be opened to visitors.

The Site Today

The car park at Barbar lies to the west of the site, where an information panel and site guard greet the visitor. There is a path running around the outside of the temple, which you join at the southwest corner. Two phases of building can be seen as you walk up to the remains of the temple – both the rubble-built walls and carved stone blocks. You should also note one of the stone altars which is immediately apparent in front of you and to the right, no longer in its original position, and behind which can be seen the three pierced 'cult stones'.

One of the best ways to view the site is to start your visit in the oval enclosure at the far side of the temple from the car park. Here the animals would have been kept tethered before being led up to the main enclosure, and here their remains were ritually burnt following the sacrifices. Follow their route to the pierced 'cult stones' where they were kept tethered, and imagine the original appearance of the great stone altar, its concave surface designed to catch the sacrificial blood. The path of the priests continues on towards the well chamber. Walk down the remains of the processional stairway, passing between the limestone plinths that once perhaps supported copper statues or standards, gleaming in the Arabian sun. Down you pass into the well chamber, remembering this was once dark and lit only by lamps in the wall niches, and that as you walked down the final steps, much worn with use, you would be entering the sacred waters, gateway to Enki's realm. To your left are the remains of the semi-circular basins, altars for his watery libations.

The Story from Archaeology

Temple I

"Nearly five thousand years ago men came to a lonely place near the northern shore of Bahrain island, close to the present-day village of Barbar, and determined that the land was sacred..." (Rice n.d.: 7).

Three successive temples were built at the Barbar site (**Fig.** 3.01). The earliest, Temple I, is now thought, based upon the pottery found at its base, to have been built at the end of the third millennium BC, in around 2,100 BC. After only a century of use it was largely demolished when the much grander Temple II replaced it. It was built on a natural low mound next to a freshwater spring, which is almost certainly the reason the temple was built on this site. Enki, the Mesopotamian god of sweet waters under the earth – the freshwater springs that are essential for life in this arid region – could be reached through this pool. It provided an entrance to the *apsû*, the Abyss of still, deep waters in which Enki dwelt in a palace "built of silver, adorned with lapis lazuli".

The excavations discovered that before any building took place a thin layer of sterile sand had been laid across the mound, ensuring the area was ritually clean. This in turn was covered with a layer of pure clay, in which were found a large number of objects placed, presumably, as foundation offerings and sealed beneath a further layer of clean sand (see **Fig.** 3.02). These offerings included nearly one hundred pottery beakers, several pottery bowls and plates, a copper vessel found with a gold band, a number of copper weapons (spearheads, axes, a dagger and knife), copper ingots, sheets and rods, a carnelian bead, and fragments of lapis lazuli and of steatite vessels. The pottery beakers were largely clustered

Fig. 3.02 Some of the pottery beakers placed in the clay foundation layer during the building of Temple I. (Photo. Moesgard Museum).

Fig. 3.03 (overleaf) The remains of one of the buildings of Temple I, thought to be a cella, or inner sanctum, found in the centre of the upper platform. The 'cult stones' from Temple II can be seen behind, as can some of the floor slabs from this second building. (Photo. Moesgard Museum).

into five groups. The weapons were clearly not made to be used as they are clumsily fashioned with weak blades, but seem to have been made as symbolic items to be given to the gods before the temple was constructed. A selection of these objects can be seen in the National Museum.

We can imagine the scene at Barbar four thousand years ago. Standing on the mound, next to the sacred spring, entry to the home of the gods, the priests pour libations from the pottery beakers and place their offerings of copper, gold and lapis lazuli into the newly laid floor of fresh clay. Enki's palace is described in the old Sumerian poems as "directed by the seven pipe songs, Given over to incantation, with pure songs", and we can imagine the chanting and playing of the priests at Barbar. The ceremonies complete, all evidence of their activities is buried beneath a new layer of clean sand and the work of building their new temple can begin.

The most extensive area of Temple I to remain is a central double-stepped platform, oval at its base and trapezoidal above. The walls of the platform were constructed of small, rough blocks of limestone in a clay mortar, surrounding a clay core. On the upper platform evidence for temple buildings was found, the plastered floors and walls of several rooms (see **Fig.** 3.03). On the eastern part of the platform, in an area not covered with buildings, were two large, shaped limestone blocks, one with a channel along its length and a series of grooves perpendicular to this. In this eastern area was also a three-tiered podium built of limestone slabs, and the bases of three circular stone altars. One of these altars can be seen at the site today, although not on its original base, and is a beautifully shaped circular block of stone, its sides polished smooth and its concave top finely grooved (see **Fig.** 3.04). Finely built drains ran from these altars.

These various stone features would all have played a role in the cult activities of the temple, and the altars,

Fig. 3.04
The great circular stone altar, first used in Temple I. Note the concave top to catch the sacrificial blood and the 'spout' down which it may have run. (Photo. Moesgard Museum).

almost certainly, were used for blood sacrifices - the throat of the sacrificial animal being slit over the top of the altar, the spilling of blood on stone a libation to the gods. The concave top of the circular altar would have collected the blood, which could have slowly run down through a possible 'spout' at the front, before being sluiced out through the drains. Hundreds of potsherds have been found at the site with one edge ground smooth on a hard surface, and it has been suggested this wear was caused by using the sherds to scrape congealed blood from the altars and surrounding floor.

The spring lay to the west of the temple buildings and platform, from which two stone staircases led down to the lower water level. Both a temple-well and pool were constructed around the original spring, which clearly formed the focus of certain temple rites. To keep the water pure, the system of drains surrounding the altars carried the sacrificial blood to the opposite side of the complex.

Temple II

After a relatively brief period of use, perhaps less than one hundred years, the original temple buildings at Barbar were demolished and a new, grander complex built on the platforms (see **Fig. 3.01**). The second temple was built, not from local uncut stone like its predecessor, but from shaped limestone ashlars brought from quarries on the island of Jiddah. Large limestone slabs were used to pave the floor of the central trapezoidal platform, which was raised by about 0.5m and was now enclosed by a 2m high retaining wall built from the square blocks. The new buildings rose above the platform in white magnificence.

The areas that had been important in Temple I, the sacred spring and the sacrificial altars, continued to be the ritual focus of the second temple, and they were joined by a third significant area, an oval enclosure built to the east of the main buildings and joined to it by a ramp. Oval structures are a common feature of Early Sumerian temples, and the one found at Barbar has been interpreted as a 'sacrificial area'. The Danish excavations found a deep layer of dark, grey ashes throughout the enclosure that contained many fragments of burnt bone. The bones were identified as cattle, sheep, goat and some fish, and were predominantly from parts of the body that carry very little meat, such as the jaw or foot (Bangsgaard 2003: 16). It is thought that the animals brought to the temple for sacrifice were kept in this oval enclosure before being led up the ramp to the main buildings and slaughtered on the altars. After the butchering of their bodies, the parts not taken away for consumption were ritually burned in the enclosure. The state of the bones and ash show that extreme heat was used to destroy them, and we know from other parts of the Middle East the very special care taken for the disposal of certain types of temple refuse (Bangsgaard 2003: 16). The Mesopotamian *Epic of Gilgamesh* relates how, when Ziusudra prepared burnt offerings to the gods in gratitude for his deliverance from the Great Flood, they "smelled the savour [and] gathered like flies around the sacrifice".

On the upper platform, around the altar area of Temple I, the remains of four large stone walls represent either the main temple building or an unroofed temple sanctuary. Measuring 18m on three of its sides and 15m on the fourth, this would have been an imposing edifice, appearing as a third step of the temple complex. Near the middle of the eastern wall, running along the east-west axis, are the remains of a double circular altar (see **Fig. 3.05**), built above the cruder altar of Temple I, and although only some of the stones remain today the structure is clearly a continuation of the circular stone altars used in the first Temple. The faces of

Fig. 3.05 (overleaf) The remains of the double circular altar of Temple II, looking at its front, polished face. (Photo. Moesgard Museum).

Fig. 3.06
The middle 'cult stone' in 1955, before the carved animal head had been lost. (Photo. Moesgard Museum).

the stones along the south side of the altar were polished, indicating this was the 'front' of the altar, and a channel drains away from the north side. To the southwest of the altar stand three 'cult stones', pierced oblong slabs that were presumably used to tether the animals brought up the ramp to be sacrificed on the altars (see **Fig.** 3.03). When first excavated, the middle 'cult stone' had a westward looking animal head (see **Fig.** 3.06), but this has since been broken off and lost.

In the north-eastern corner of the building long stone beams marked the edge of a 2m by 2m square 'pit of offering'. Buried in the pit were a spectacular collection of objects: several alabaster vases or jars, a copper mirror handle in the shape of a man (see **Fig.** 3.07), a copper bird, various odd pieces of copper and lapis-lazuli beads. Also buried nearby was the most famous object found at Barbar, a

Fig. 3.07
The copper mirror
handle found in the
'pit of offering' of
Temple II. The mirror
would have originally
been attached to
the figure's feet.
Similar objects are
known from southern
Uzbekistan and
northern Afghanistan,
though this piece
could have been
locally made. (Photo.
Moesgard Museum).

small copper bull's head (see **Fig.** 3.08), together with a number of copper sheets, nails and circular bands. Holes had been punched into the largest sheet. These copper objects have been interpreted as the remains of a lyre, similar to those found in the Royal Graves of Ur, the wood having rotted away leaving the copper sheets which covered the sounding box and the bull's head which would have adorned it. Lyres with bulls' heads appear on Dilmun stamp seals found on Failaka, an island off the coast of Kuwait. The lyre appears to have been buried during the construction of Temple II. These remarkable objects are displayed in the National Museum.

A 30-step staircase 15m long and almost 2m wide, built from large shaped limestone blocks, ran down from the upper platform to the basin built around the spring. Unfortunately, only part of the staircase is preserved today, but it must have been so impressive when the Temple was in use that it has been described as a "processional stairway" by Danish archaeologists (Andersen and Højlund 2003). It ran down from above ground-level on the central platform, through a portal, to below ground-level at the basin, where the final three steps ended below the original water-level. A double row of large limestone plinths flanked the staircase at the foot of the central platform, one of them decorated with a carving of human figures (see **Fig.** 3.09). The plinths all have two vertical rectangular holes and traces of wood, copper and bitumen were found in the holes of three of the plinths suggesting that copper-covered wooden objects had been mounted in them, perhaps statues or standards.

In this second Temple the pool chamber was divided into two rooms, a western and eastern room. The western room contained the pool proper and it was here that the staircase ended (see **Fig.** 3.10). In the southeast corner of the pool is a well-

Fig. 3.08 (opposite) The copper bull's head found in the 'pit of offering' of Temple II. It is thought to have been a decorative part of a lyre. (Photo. Moesgard Museum).

Fig. 3.09
The decorated limestone plinth placed at the bottom of the processional stairway of Temple II. It is carved with representations of human figures. The holes carved in the top would originally have supported important objects, perhaps religious statues or standards. (Photo. Moesgard Museum).

like basin, formed from two immense semicircular hollow stone drums, and on a plinth beside it was a stone vessel. Holes in the walls of this stone jar suggest it was partially submerged in the water – the holes allowing water to flow into, and out of, it. A niche in the wall may have held a light. We can imagine the temple in use; the priests descend the great staircase, chanting to the gods. Passing from the sunlight above they walk through the portal, between the standards, and down into the dark depths of the pool chamber, lit only by the flickering of lamps. Perhaps they walk down the final steps into the cool water, standing in the gateway of Enki, and solemnly pouring libations of his holy water at the great stone altars.

Fig. 3.10 (Page 65) The western pool room of Temple II. The staircase can be seen on the left, descending into the water, the semi-circular basin is on the right, and the pierced stone vessel is on the plinth between. (Photo. Moesgard Museum).

Temple III and the North-Eastern Temple

Like the original temple, the second complex was also replaced after a relatively brief period of time, perhaps after only a century. The final temple complex, Temple III, marks a change in the use and rituals of the site and the spiritually important areas, the pool, the Eastern court containing the altars, and the oval sacrificial enclosure, were all covered over. The destruction of such important areas both marks a deliberate end of past practices, and also shows a degree of reverence as the demolition and subsequent remodelling were clearly done with respect. The new structures appear to have been even larger and more magnificent than those they replaced. The new central platform completely covered the platform of Temple II, and its shape was changed from trapezoid to a square 38m by 38m. However, in the four thousand years that have passed since the walls were first raised, the stones have been removed, block by block, for use elsewhere, leaving us mainly with foundations as evidence.

Although the pool of Temple II was now covered over, the freshwater spring that had originally inspired the construction of Barbar temple continued to be of religious importance. A new well was constructed in the southwest corner, over the remains of an earlier well that may date back to the original temple. It is built from stone drums which abut the wall, and presumably rose all the way through the platform to the central building, an impressive piece of engineering.

Some 15m to the northeast of the Barbar Temple mound lay a smaller, lower tell. This tell contained the remains of a double terrace, two platforms one above the other, contemporary with Temple III. The upper platform, like that of Temple III, was a perfect square, measuring 24m by 24m. A very

Fig. 3.11
The foot and handprints of the builders of the north-eastern temple, preserved for four thousand years. (Photo. Moesgard Museum).

large building once stood upon this platform, of which every stone has since been removed by stone-robbers. A deep hole had been dug in the centre of the tell by the stone-robbers, down below the foundation level, suggesting the presence of a well chamber similar to that of the main temple.

The most interesting discovery at the north-eastern temple was found in the foundation layer in the southeastern corner. The whole area inside the inner wall here had been used when the foundations were newly laid and was clearly marked with human foot and handprints (see **Fig.** 3.11), together with the impressions of reed mats. This foundation layer had been covered by the fill of the upper platform, preserving the prints of the builders for four thousand years.

The construction of a second, smaller and lower temple to the northeast of the main temple has been interpreted by the Danish archaeologists as reflecting a change in practices of worship at Barbar (Andersen and Højlund 2003: 208). Together with the remodelling of the main temple and the covering of previously important areas, the double-temple site is seen as a major change in religious conception. It was to be the final change at Barbar, which appears to have fallen into disuse a hundred years later.

Chapter Four

The Burial Mounds

"the greatest curiosity of Bahrein"

Theodore Bent, presenting a paper on Bahrain to the Royal Geographic Society in London in 1889 introduced his learned audience to "the greatest curiosity of Bahrein...namely, the vast sea of sepulchral mounds...a vast necropolis of some unknown race" (Bent, quoted in Rice 1984: 80-81). Important and fascinating as the other archaeological sites of Bahrain are, it is the great fields of burial mounds which once covered mile after mile that are the most truly astounding. It has been estimated that there were originally 170,000 burial mounds on the main island, so numerous and built so closely together that one might think "the rugged surface is due to a natural phenomenon, a seething mass of sand, stiffened at the beginning of time and not the work of man" (Glob 1968: 14). The Bahrain cemeteries are thought to be the greatest concentration of burial mounds found anywhere in the world today (see **Fig.** 4.01). The tombs date from the Early Dilmun period, the days of the first city at Qala'at al-Bahrain and the temple at Barbar, and are found in the north and west of the island in the area of desert that stretches between the fertile coastal strip and the central depression.

Although the incredible rate of development of Bahrain has meant that many mounds are now gone, covered by modern urbanisation, the tombs that remain are still impressive. In particular, the so called 'Royal' mounds (see **Fig.** 4.02 and **Fig.** 4.03), a group of much larger tombs which dominate the skyline of A'ali village, can still affect the visitor

Fig. 4.01 (overleaf) Danish excavations at A'ali in 1963. The sea of mounds stretches to the horizon. (Photo. Moesgard Museum).

Fig. 4.03
Lime burning amidst the 'Royal' mounds at A'ali, c. 1960. (Photo. Moesgard Museum).

Fig. 4.02 (opposite)
One of the 'Royal' mounds at A'ali, photographed during an early Danish expedition. (Photo. Moesgard Museum).

today as they once affected Theodore Bent in the nineteenth century. Fortunately for archaeology, before their destruction many of the tombs were excavated by the National Museum of Bahrain, and in 2009 the Bahraini authorities submitted an application to Unesco to have 11 mound sites containing 12,000 graves placed on the World Heritage List. The endless panoramas shown in early photographs may no longer exist, but it is still possible for the visitor today to stand amidst the monuments to those long dead in one of the greatest cemeteries that were ever built.

Directions to Site

The best mounds to visit are the Royal Mounds at A'ali, and the remains of the burial field there. Follow the signs for A'ali Pottery from the main Sheikh Khalifa Bin Salman Highway. It is easiest to park outside the potteries, one of which has been built into a large mound, and visit the mounds on foot. The village of A'ali surrounds many of the Royal Mounds and a walk around the streets will encounter several of them. Opposite the Delmon Pottery, for example, is a collapsed mound in which the original drum structure is clearly visible. To get to the main mound field continue down Ave 71 past the potteries, past the large mosque, for about 100m. A large mound will be visible on the opposite side of the road. At the small roundabout turn left and head down the side alley that will take you to the edge of the remaining mound field.

Past Research

Unlike some of the archaeological sites found on Bahrain, which have lain hidden beneath the sands until careful excavation revealed their true importance, the "vast sea" of burial mounds dominates the landscape (see **Fig.** 4.04). Archaeologists have been recording and exploring them since Captain Durand gave his first report on a visit made in 1878, writing that "mighty mounds bare of vegetation tower above the palm groves. Mass upon mass, mound upon mound, they stretch on in endless chains all round the slope that falls from the cliffs to the sea" (Durand, in Rice 1984: 17). Consequently, there is a much greater history of archaeological work on the burial mounds than on any other site in Bahrain.

Durand identified the smaller mounds as "unquestionably graves", but hoped that the larger mounds he found at A'ali might prove to be temples.

Fig. 4.04 (opposite) Aerial photo taken in 1959, showing the density of burial mounds that then existed. (Photo. Moesgard Museum).

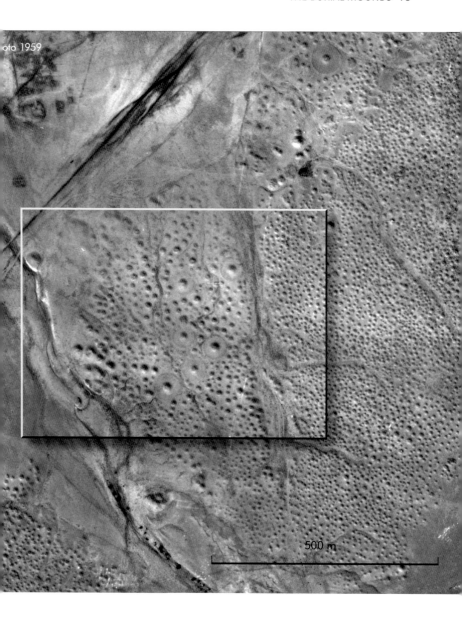

oto 1959

500 m

To further examine this theory he searched for a way into the heart of the mounds and, "at last my perseverance was rewarded by finding an entrance into one of these (under a flat stone near the summit), through which, lying down, we were just able to creep, and on getting beyond the opening we found ourselves in a long passage or gallery, which was, however, blocked with fallen masonry a few yards in front of us." (Rice 1984: 23). His explorations halted, Durand excavated one of the small mounds, in which he found skeletal remains, and, in the following year, one of the large mounds at A'ali, concluding that both were types of tomb.

In 1889 the mound fields, "the greatest curiosity of Bahrein", drew Mr and Mrs Theodore Bent, the explorer/travel-writing couple, to the islands. They too concentrated on the large mounds at A'ali, pitching their tents in the shadow of one of them. A very early photograph shows Mr Bent dressed in a peculiarly British outfit of deer-stalker hat and tweeds, entertaining Bahraini dignitaries at the mounds. Their excavations recovered a variety of objects: ivory, pottery and metals, the quality of which confirmed them in the erroneous belief that these were the tombs of Phoenicians.

The first scientific excavations of the mounds were begun in 1906 by the incumbent British Political Resident himself, Colonel F.B. Prideaux. In 1904 the Director General of the Archaeological Department of the Government of India had announced his intention of visiting Bahrain to settle "the question of the origin of the necropolis". The visit did not happen, but instead 1,600 rupees were sent to Prideaux to fund the work. He also camped at A'ali, returning to his office in Manama on the weekly mail-days to deal with his political duties. Although the rupees ran out after just one season, Prideaux worked with military speed excavating seven large or medium mounds and twenty-five small mounds, often driving tunnels directly through the hard gravel conglomerate to the central chamber. In total Prideaux was to excavate sixty-seven tumuli, his reports being accompanied by a number of photographs and a plan of the principal A'ali tombs. He recovered a variety of finds, including two gold rings and fragments of two ivory statuettes that were sent to the British Museum for identification. The museum experts suggested these resembled ivories mistakenly believed to be Phoenician, thus reinforcing the Phoenician theory suggested by the Bents.

Ernest Mackay, encouraged to visit Bahrain by the great Egyptologist Flinders Petrie, arrived in 1925 to determine "the nature of the tombs and their contents". He also concentrated his work at A'ali, opening thirty-four tombs, of which he believed twenty to have been undamaged by looters. Human remains were found in twenty-one mounds, conditions being too damp for preservation in several cases, and a variety of grave goods were recorded, including bronze objects or fragments from nearly every tomb and a quantity of ivory, most notably a broken female figurine. The first professional archaeologist to work on the mounds, Mackay wrote an excellent report of his work, including an analysis of the different construction methods and a number of plans and photographs, which was published by the Egypt Exploration Society.

In late 1940 and early 1941, an American graduate student, Peter B. Cornwall, excavated a further thirty mounds. He sent much of the material he found back to America for later study and publication, including the skeletal remains that came to be deposited as the Cornwall Collection at the Hearst Museum of Anthropology, UC Berkeley. This Collection is now the focus of the Dilmun Bioarchaeology Project, a joint team of

Fig. 4.05
P.V. Glob excavating a
burial mound in the
Saar Burial Field, 1954.
(Photo. Moesgard
Museum).

scholars from UC Berkeley and Sonoma State University specialising in skeletal analysis, which promises to greatly increase our knowledge of the people who were buried in these tombs. Their eventual aim to attempt the facial reconstruction of three individuals will even enable us to "come face to face" with these Bahrainis of long ago.

The incredible number of burial mounds had caused all those who gazed upon them to wonder, "if these miles upon miles of crowded heaps are tombs, where did the inhabitants live?" (Durand 1880, quoted in Rice 1984: 22). There were two main theories, both suggested initially by Capt. Durand: either people had lived along the coast, or Bahrain was an Island of the Dead, a cemetery for those dwelling on the mainland. No one theory dominated, although Mackay argued forcefully that, "it is probable that there was not a large enough population in ancient days to account for the enormous number of tumuli on the island... we must conclude that the people who were buried on Bahrein were brought from some part of the mainland" (quoted in Rice 1984: 158). The Danish Archaeological Expedition that arrived in Bahrain in 1953, however, finally provided a much clearer picture of the tomb builders. Drawn to Bahrain by the great sea of tombs, unlike their predecessors Geoffrey Bibby and P.V. Glob did not come primarily to excavate mounds but with the aim of discovering a more complete picture of the prehistory of Bahrain and a clearer idea of Bahrain's place in world history. They did excavate two mounds in their first season (see **Fig.** 4.05), but it was the discovery of contemporary settlement at Qala'at al-Bahrain and of the temple at Barbar that was the focus of their work, and which was to provide the first clear picture of the society whose dead lay buried in the many thousands of tombs.

The Danish archaeological relationship with Bahrain has proved to be an enduring one. In the years since Bibby and Glob first drove out to A'ali in an old Humber station-wagon bought for 170 dollars from Bapco (Bahrain Petroleum Company), Danish researchers have continued to explore the mounds and to broaden our knowledge of this past society. Today, the Oriental Department of Moesgaard Museum in collaboration with the Bahrain Directorate for Culture and National Heritage is running a project to map the burial mounds of Bahrain using aerial photographs from 1959 and historic maps (see **Fig.** 4.06). The resulting plans are being used to learn more about the development of the cemeteries and the society that created them.

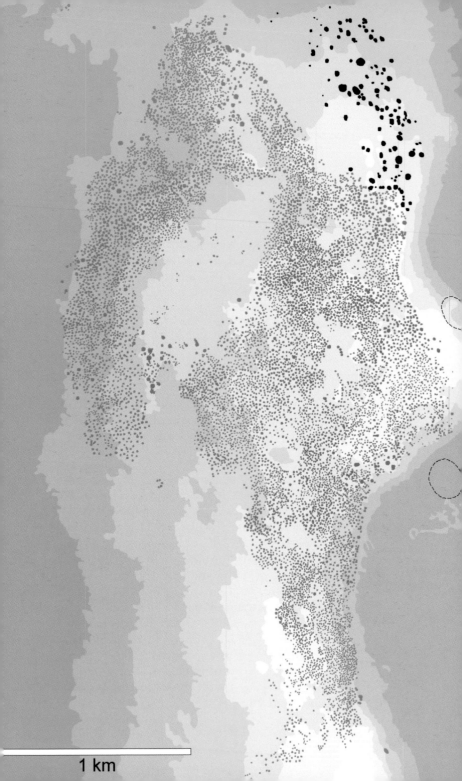

1 km

The rapid pace of economic and social development in Bahrain has meant that since the 1960s many of the mounds have had to be removed to allow for urban expansion. Before their destruction, a large number, perhaps 8,000, were excavated by the National Museum of Bahrain and by various foreign missions, of which less than 300 have been published. However, this relatively large body of data does provide us with a fair overview of the "way of death" of those who once lay buried in the "vast sea of sepulchral mounds".

The Site Today

The burial mounds we see today have collapsed and eroded over the centuries, changing slowly from stone-walled drums to rubble mounds. It is rewarding just to wander around the A'ali mounds, imagining how Bahrain appeared just a few decades ago when these burial fields stretched for mile after mile, the greatest concentration of burial mounds in the world. However, for those particularly interested in their original structure there are some clues to be found. Parking by the A'ali potteries, walk around to the Delmon pottery on the far right of the row where a large mound on the opposite side of the road clearly shows the drum-like structure within the heart of the later erosion.

Fig. 4.06 (opposite) Burial mounds recorded at Saar. Danish archaeologist Steffen Terp Laursen is collating various sources to produce these plans. (Image Moesgard Museum).

There is also a large mound in the main mound field in which the original chambers can be seen (**Fig.** 4.07). Follow the instructions given in the Directions section to reach the main mound field and this mound should be obvious – it is very large and not too far from the road, and past excavations have left it 'hollowed out'. Whilst visiting the mound field take the trouble to climb to the top of the highest mound for a view that encompasses ancient Bahrain, the burial mounds, traditional Bahrain, A'ali village, and modern Bahrain, the high-rise buildings of Manama (see **Fig.** 4.08).

Fig. 4.07 (overleaf) Entrances to the chambers in one of the 'Royal' mounds at A'ali. (Photo. Insoll and MacLean).

Fig. 4.08 Ancient and modern Bahrain – a 'Royal' burial mound next to a village house in A'ali today. (Photo. Insoll and MacLean).

Finally, at the site of Saar (see the following chapter) archaeologists have rebuilt a Dilmun period tomb so that visitors may have a greater idea how they once appeared. Once at the site of Saar, the tomb can be reached by walking to the far western end of the site.

Good recreations of the contents of the graves revealed during excavation can be found in the National Museum's Hall of Graves.

The Story from Archaeology

Life and Death in Early Dilmun

Although the Bahrain burial mounds are resting places of the dead, they are able to tell us a great deal about the living society that constructed them. From the first, scattered tombs built above small villages to vast cemeteries serving the thriving, cosmopolitan 'Capital of Dilmun', the nature of Bahraini society four thousand years ago can be

Fig. 4.09
Skeleton lying in a
burial chamber, Umm
Jidr cemetery 1965.
(Photo. Moesgard
Museum).

seen in the way the dead were buried - where and how their tombs were built, and the personal possessions they took with them. These are the tombs of individuals who once lived and worked in Bahrain, men, women and children. After death they were placed inside pre-built stone chambers, lying on one side, their head to the north, legs bent and their hands resting by or under their face (see **Fig.** 4.09). Accompanying them were objects from their lives – pots, small baskets of food, ostrich eggshells used for drinking vessels and personal ornaments. Following the funeral rituals the chamber was sealed, the dead were left in the

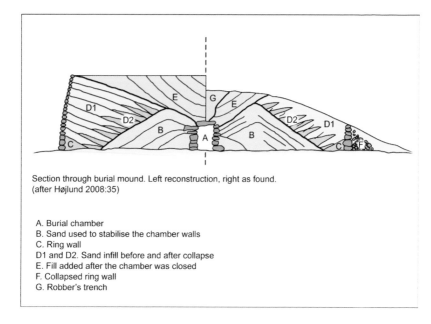

Section through burial mound. Left reconstruction, right as found.
(after Højlund 2008:35)

A. Burial chamber
B. Sand used to stabilise the chamber walls
C. Ring wall
D1 and D2. Sand infill before and after collapse
E. Fill added after the chamber was closed
F. Collapsed ring wall
G. Robber's trench

Fig. 4.10
Plan showing the
original drum-like
construction of a burial
and its subsequent
collapse into a mound.

peace of the tomb and the living returned to their
everyday lives.

The strange lunar landscape we see today is not
how the mounds would have originally appeared.
Excavation has shown that they are in fact highly
eroded monuments, and their original shape has
been the subject of a long debate. General consensus
now agrees with the arguments of the German
archaeologist Christian Velde. After a careful
consideration of the effect of 4,000 years of wind
and rain and the current pattern of collapsed ring
walls and the stone and sand infill he concluded that
the tombs were once surrounded by almost vertical
ring-walls. They were drum-like in appearance,
rather than mounds (see **Fig.** 4.10 and **Fig.** 4.11).
In 1993 the London-Bahrain Archaeological
Expedition rebuilt a burial with four shaft graves
at the site of Saar. From the way the stones in the
ring wall had fallen they too came to the conclusion

Fig. 4.11
Partially excavated
burial mound
showing the original
construction wall, Saar
village. (Photo. Insoll
and MacLean).

that the tomb had not been a 'mound', but rather an aboveground structure. The rebuilt tomb can be visited today, and modern gaps in the wall allow a glimpse of the shaft burials below. It gives a good idea of how the burials appeared to the Bahraini communities who built and used them; they lived in a landscape of circular stone walls, not of sandy mounds.

The mounds now look deceptively similar, but it was quickly apparent to archaeologists that the tombs were not all built in the same way and that over time the method of construction had changed (see **Fig.** 4.12). The tombs can be divided into two main groups, the Early and the Late Type. The first

Fig. 4.12
Excavation of a
mound at A'ali, 1963,
revealing the original
construction. (Photo.
Moesgard Museum).

mounds have been dated, based upon imported ceramics found in the graves, to 2250-2050 BC, and are typically low with a flat top, characterised by a rock fill between the burial chamber and the outer wall and by a lack of capstones. The Late Type mounds are bigger, typically two to three times the size of the Early Type Mounds, and display a much greater variety of size and of chamber layout. They are more conical in appearance, generally having capstones covering a central chamber and an earth or gravel fill between the chamber and the outer wall. These Late Type mounds have been dated to the period 2050-1800 BC. The very large mounds at A'ali, the 'Royal' mounds, are of this Late Type.

One of the other most noticeable differences between the Early and Late Type mounds is in their location, and in the concentration of the Late Type mounds in cemeteries. The earlier, smaller tombs are scattered in a broad, crescent shaped area around Rifa'a, on the slopes of the island's central limestone

Fig. 4.13 (opposite)
The mound fields, or
cemeteries, of Ancient
Bahrain.

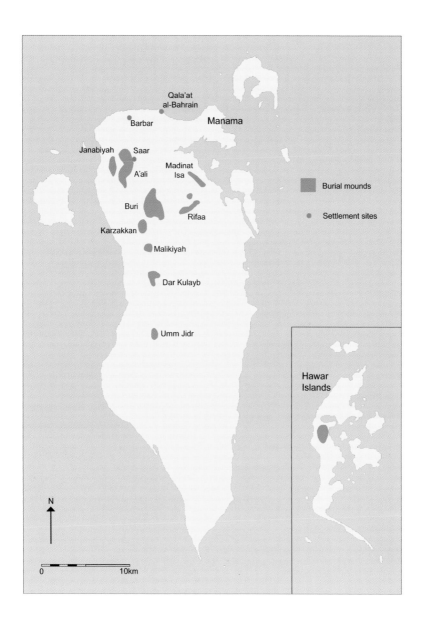

Qala'at
al-Bahrain

Barbar

Manama

Janabiyah   Saar

Madinat
A'ali   Isa

Buri

Rifaa

Karzakkan

Malikiyah

Dar Kulayb

Umm Jidr

Burial mounds

Settlement sites

Hawar
Islands

N

0   10km

dome and are generally found on the banks of old, dry, fossil wadis. In contrast, the later tombs are clustered together in ten vast cemeteries (see **Fig. 4.13**). They are also built upon the limestone, but generally lower down the slope than the older tombs. All the mounds were built on poor land, above the springs and the areas where the modern villages and farms are found.

The change over time in tomb numbers, construction methods, and in where the tombs were built can tell us about the changing nature of Bahraini society, something that Danish archaeologists in particular, such as Flemming Højlund and Steffen Terp Laursen, have studied. The ongoing Bahraini/Danish Bahrain Burial Mound Project has, to date, managed to map over 75,000 mounds – 28,000 Early Type, and 47,000 Late Type, and they have used these figures to calculate the estimated past population of Bahrain. They suggest that a population of around 9,000 – 10,500 people were living on Bahrain when the Early Type tombs were built, that is 2250-2050 BC, but that in the period when the Later Type tombs were built, 2050-1800 BC, the population increased by over 30% to 12,000-14,000 people (Laursen: in press).

With the growth in population came social and economic changes. The early graves are small and relatively simple. They represent the burial of individuals living in small villages and with a relatively egalitarian status. The later graves show a change. As the villages became larger, the graves became more numerous and clustered in large cemeteries, and we begin to see the development of a more complex society. Burials become more differentiated – the size of the grave and the amount and quality of the grave goods show that some individuals were now much wealthier or more important than others. It is only in these later tombs that we find stamp-seals (see the section on seals). These valuable and symbolic objects have frequently been found lying at the neck of both adults and children, showing they had been buried wearing them.

The Stamp Seals of Bahrain

Seals have been used throughout history to authorise business transactions and to prevent tampering with containers of goods. A distinctive design is carved into a seal which, when impressed upon a piece of damp clay, leaves an impression unique to its owner. Seals first appear in Bahrain during the Dilmun period - the earliest securely dated seals being found at Qala'at al-Bahrain and dating to 2200-2100 BC. They were in use on the island for more than 500 years.

Seals were common at this time in the great trading centres with which Bahrain was tied, Mesopotamia, Assyria and the Indus Valley civilizations. The seals that appear on Bahrain have, in some cases, elements similar to seals from all these areas, showing again Bahrain's pivotal role in these great trade networks. However, the people of Dilmun created their own distinctive style, producing seals in local workshops for use in their own island economy as well as their international trade.

The Bahraini seals are circular stamp seals made from stone, often steatite, though with rare examples in ivory or pottery. A design is carved on one side and a perforation bored through the reverse so that they could be worn or carried on a thong or string.

The images carved on them provide us with many tiny windows into this ancient world. They include a variety of animals, particularly an elegant gazelle-like creature, insects and birds, human figures and symbols. The humans shown are nearly all male. Some have beards, some wear hemispherical caps, some wear long tiered skirts, others carry shields or weapons. We see them hunting, riding horses, drinking through straws, weaving. There is even a seal that shows a seated figure holding a pan balance of a type that is still used by pearl merchants in the Gulf today.

The excavations at Saar recovered ninety-five seals and seal fragments and these were the subject of a study by Dr Harriet Crawford. She was able to conclude from their wide distribution at Saar that seals were not only used by an elite, but were owned and used by many members of the community. Seals have also been found in the graves of children and adults, some of which appear to be women, implying that they may have had more than a simple economic purpose. Crawford suggests that children may have been given seals to wear as amulets, for protection, later, as adults, using their seals for business purposes.

For further information see Harriet Crawford's excellent book *Early Dilmun Seals from Saar* (2001).

Recently, Laursen has identified a third, and much rarer, type of mound that he has called a 'ring mound' or Radial Wall Type (Laursen 2008). As the name suggests, these mounds are characterised by the presence of an outer ring wall built of limestone blocks, which is typically twice or more the diameter of the mound it surrounds. The ring mounds tend to be large and include the 'Royal' mounds at A'ali. However, outside of the A'ali cemetery, all the ring mounds recorded appear with scatters of Early Type mounds. Laursen has convincingly argued that the ring mounds are the tombs of a social elite, and that in the earlier period, 2250-2050 BC, power was

Fig. 4.14
Excavation in progress
of a 'Royal' mound at
A'ali, 1963. (Photo.
Moesgard Museum).

decentralised – the smaller, scattered communities each had a local hierarchy. However, as Bahraini society became more developed, power struggles between the various elites for control of the trade market led to the collapse of the old system. In their place emerged a single ruling lineage whose ring mound tombs are found in the A'ali cemetery.

The rise of this one high authority is clearly linked with the appearance of the first Bahraini city and its monumental buildings, the palace and warehouses that represent political and economic control, and also with the first temple at Barbar, centre of religious power. This was a truly dynamic period in Bahrain. Laursen has also argued that these changes are connected to the rise of Dilmun as a trading power. At the end of the third millennium BC Dilmun took control of the lucrative copper trade, replacing Magan (source of copper ore) which had been the principal trading partner of Mesopotamia. This changing relationship is reflected in the pottery recovered from the burial mounds. In the Early Type tombs we find Umm an-Nar pottery imported from Magan, in the later cemeteries it quickly fades away. The new ruling dynasty in Dilmun displayed its power and wealth in the size and dominance of its tombs, the 'Royal' tombs at A'ali do indeed seem to be 'Royal'. The Mari archives, a vast collection of tablets in Akkadian found in the ancient city of Mari in modern Syria, describe the sending of gifts of oil and a special jar to a King of Dilmun during the reign of Shamshi-Adad(c. 1813-1781 BC). It is possible that the body of this very King once lay in a Royal Mound at A'ali (see **Fig.** 4.14).

Chapter Five

Saar

Outside the modern village of Saar, next to the main highway to Saudi Arabia, lies a much earlier village. The old village at Saar dates from the Early Dilmun period four thousand years ago, yet its wall foundations are so well preserved that it is possible to walk down its main street and through the doors of its houses. When the ships carrying precious cargos from India, Africa and Mesopotamia were safely harboured at the great trading city at Qala'at al-Bahrain, villagers at Saar were living a more simple life, fishing, farming and hunting. Yet they too were tied into these exotic trade networks, as finds by archaeologists have shown. Even in the villages these early Bahrainis were playing a part in the wider world.

Directions to Site

The archaeological site of Saar is to the north of the Sheikh Isa Bin Salman Highway. There is a sign on the Highway directing you north at the junction with the Janabiyah Highway – do not miss it and end up on the King Fahad Causeway to Saudi Arabia. Shortly after leaving the main Highway you need to take the first road on the right, again indicated by a sign, and continue on the tarmac until you reach a dirt road. Turn right again and a brown sign is visible at the site entrance ahead. Entrance is free.

Past Research

In 1989 the London-Bahrain Archaeological Expedition, directed by Robert Killick and Jane

Moon, came to Bahrain with the sole aim of locating and excavating an Early Dilmun settlement. At this time, most evidence of Dilmun period Bahrain came from the burial mounds, from religious sites such as Barbar temple, and from the city at Qala'at al-Bahrain. There was very little evidence of how ordinary villagers lived their day-to-day lives. Together with Bahraini colleagues, particularly those from the Bahrain National Museum, they visited various potential sites searching for evidence of a Dilmun period settlement that was both easily accessible and with a great enough depth and extent of material to allow the extensive and thorough study they planned. Bahraini archaeologists, led by Dr Moawiyah Ibrahim, had been excavating a burial complex near the village of Saar prior to the building of the causeway to Saudi Arabia when they uncovered the remains of a temple and other buildings. The site was then sampled in 1983 and 1985 by an Arab team led by Dr Hussein Kandil, and the pottery they found enabled the site to be dated as Early Dilmun. Visiting Saar, Killick and Moon immediately realised its archaeological potential and the London-Bahrain Archaeological Expedition began excavations there on 3rd March 1990. They were to continue work at the site for nearly ten years, finally finishing on 13th May 1999.

The London-Bahrain Archaeological Expedition succeeded in enthusing Bahraini and non-Bahraini alike with interest in Bahrain's past. The project involved professionals from Britain and Bahrain, and relied upon a very dedicated group of volunteers who not only worked on the excavations, but also led guided tours for the frequent visitors and educational groups. It was the first excavation in recent times to employ Bahraini workmen, a practice which has now become common. Financial support was provided by the British and Bahraini states, but also by a great number of businesses and individuals in

Fig. 5.01 (opposite) Excavations in progress at Saar, the project involved professionals and volunteers from Britain and Bahrain. Here they are excavating a terrace of houses. (Photo. courtesy of the Bahrain Ministry of Culture and Information).

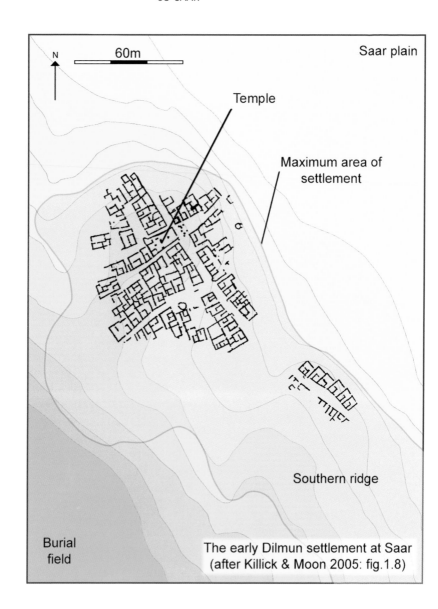

N

60m

Saar plain

Temple

Maximum area of
settlement

Southern ridge

Burial
field

The early Dilmun settlement at Saar
(after Killick & Moon 2005: fig.1.8)

Bahrain. This unprecedented level of involvement led to a truly impressive ten-year project that was able to investigate thoroughly this well-preserved site (see **Fig.** 5.01). Not only was it painstakingly excavated, it was also comprehensively published by Killick and Moon and their co-director Harriet Crawford (see particularly Killick and Moon 2005; and Crawford, Killick and Moon 1997; Crawford 2001), providing us with a very clear picture of village life in Saar four thousand years ago.

The Site Today

The car park at the site of Saar lies next to the old site offices used during the excavations, and you walk past these and down the slope to reach the village. The Main Street of the old settlement runs across in front of you, the housing blocks largely clustered along its length (see **Fig.** 5.02). The temple lies towards the northern end of the street, to the left of the car park, and it is probably best to begin your tour here. The remains of the columns that once supported the roof can be clearly seen, as can the altars with their crescent shaped backs. Try to imagine the building interior as it once was, dark and hidden, with its crimson walls and the smell of burnt offerings and incense lingering around its altars. From the temple you can wander up and down the Main Street and side alleys, exploring the small houses. Look out for any remaining features – wall niches can be seen in a house near the temple, and a basin in a house at the other end of the settlement.

At the southern end of the site – back down Main Street, past the car park, and close to the highway – some of the honeycomb burials can be seen. Take time to visit the drum-shaped burial that was reconstructed by the London-Bahrain Archaeological Expedition in 1993. This is how all the burial mounds would once have appeared,

Fig. 5.02
Plan of the Dilmun period village found at Saar.

a very different landscape of thousands of drums rather than the mound fields we are left with today.

The Story from Archaeology

The Saar excavations revealed an intact Early Dilmun period village complete with a main street, housing blocks and temple (see **Fig.** 5.02). The settlement is built upon a small eastern outcrop of the limestone ridge that runs across northern Bahrain, and looks east to Tubli Bay and south across land that was once desert to A'ali. Until relatively recently an inlet stretched inland from the east coast to within 3.6km of the site and may have been much closer when the village was built, providing safe anchorage below the ridge. Fresh water was drawn by the villagers from a well found in the north-west corner of the site. To the west and south of the village is a large mound-field, and a distinctive 'honeycomb' style cemetery was found to the south, both contemporary with the village.

The 'Main Street' at Saar was approximately 200m long and 5m wide and ran from the northwest of the site to the southeast. Only a few streets and alleys lead off it, and the excavators used these to divide the village into five main areas or 'quarters'. These quarters were made up of housing blocks – groups of houses sharing common walls and either separated by open space or distinguished from each other by differing orientation. About 80 houses were uncovered by the excavations and, as less than half the site was excavated, it is probable that there were approximately 200 houses in the village. From the range of evidence found we know a great deal about the lives of these early Bahrainis, what they ate, how they cooked, how they may have occupied their leisure time, and where and how they were buried when they died.

Village Life at Saar

The houses we see today actually reflect the third phase of the site when most of the blocks were rebuilt. The earliest evidence for occupation at Saar was found below the centre of the site and was dated, from the pottery recovered, to the end of the third millennium BC and the start of the second millennium BC. It was during the second phase of occupation that the roads were laid out, most of the housing blocks were first constructed and the temple erected. This initial building phase was relatively rapid, reflecting a considerable expansion and development of the site in the first century of the second millennium BC (ca. 2000-1950 BC). In the third phase of occupation the whole village underwent a major rebuild, although generally the same house and block boundaries continued to be used. The rebuild was not one single event, but rather a series of individual building projects over a generation or two. The village continued to be inhabited for one-two hundred years before, in the fourth phase of occupation, it shrank rapidly, being finally abandoned in the eighteenth century BC.

The blocks of houses are laid out with some regularity, suggesting a degree of overall planning, and the houses themselves generally conform to a standard plan. There is not a single detached house in the village. All the houses are built in blocks, sharing communal walls, either in rows of identical buildings, or as variations of a basic theme – they are prehistoric terraced homes (see **Fig.** 5.01). Entering most of these houses you walk in from the street down a narrow passage into a large room, from which a rear exit leads to the outside. Built into a corner of the main room, generally to the left of the entrance, is an inner rectangular room. The door to the inner room is nearly always out of sight of the main entrance. Although a few houses have a third, or even a fourth, room, the private inner room is common to all.

We have a good idea how the houses at Saar once appeared from the walls and residue that now remain. The walls are built of rough limestone, but this would have originally been plastered, possibly with some moulded plaster decoration. The houses appear to have been single storey with roofs of palm-leaf or reed tied to palm beams – we know this from fragments of roof plaster bearing impressions of reeds and palm leaves. It is possible that some of these roofs were used as extra storage or living space. Some of the larger houses may also have had an open courtyard. The impressions of woven-palm leaves also suggest that woven mats covered at least some of the floors. Recesses by some of the doorjambs show that doors were used, and that they may have had basic locking bars, but there is no evidence for any windows. A good model of a typical Saar house can be seen in the National Museum.

Using a variety of archaeological evidence, including the detailed study of some house floors (micromorphology), we also know how the villagers lived in their homes. The private inner rooms show little evidence of household activities, there is no general domestic debris for instance. Instead, they appear to have been used for storage (for example, 13 fragments of clay sealings were found in one of these rooms) and for sitting and sleeping. The faunal evidence also suggests that these rooms were more likely to be used for eating red meat, perhaps a higher status food served to guests or eaten on special occasions, and so these rooms may have been used for entertaining.

The outer rooms, in contrast, were used for all the daily household chores, "these were always the rooms with the dirty floors" write Killick and Moon (2005: 347). In these outer rooms we find not only the debris from the preparation of many past meals, but also a range of common built-

Fig. 5.03
Kitchen area in the corner of a Saar house. A circular hearth, cooking pot supports and tannur oven can be seen. (Photo. courtesy of the Bahrain Ministry of Culture and Information).

in kitchen facilities: ovens, hearths, cooking pot supports, storage bins, vats and pits, and basins, the prehistoric equivalent of a fitted kitchen (see **Fig. 5.03**).

The *tannur*, a circular clay-lined oven that uses a minimal amount of fuel to reach very high temperatures, is found today throughout North Africa and the Middle East and has been in use for at least five thousand years. It is mainly used for baking unleavened bread – the round flat loaves of dough being slapped onto the interior walls of the oven where the intense heat bakes them within a minute. Thirty-five of these *tannur* bread ovens were found built into the houses at Saar, either against the wall or in a corner of the main room, still, in many cases, containing a layer of fine grey ash left by the daily baking four thousand years earlier (see **Fig. 5.04**).

The domestic cooks of Saar had a considerable repertoire. They not only baked in their kitchens,

Fig. 5.04
One of the tannur ovens found at Saar, its internal wall blackened from years of baking bread. (Photo. courtesy of the Bahrain Ministry of Culture and Information).

they also stewed, grilled and possibly roasted. Various types of hearths and fire-pits are found in the houses: thirty-one semicircular hearths, twelve ring hearths, fifty-four fire-pits and seven vertical-sided fire-pits. The hearths have a plastered lip that separates them from the surrounding floor, and an interior that has been baked hard through repeated use and replastered on several occasions. Like the ovens, they are built into the main outer rooms of houses, sometimes as part of a cooking suite with the oven and a cooking pot support. They were identified by the excavators as the basic cooking mechanism of every household, used for boiling liquids, stewing and grilling, and the cooking of these many, various meals has left traces of burning on the walls and floors that surround them, and the remains of ash in the hearths themselves. The fire-pits are less sophisticated, simply shallow scoops in the ground showing signs of burning. Some of these may represent only a single fire, but others were clearly heavily used and one contained a permanent cooking-pot support made from a broken jar rim supported by stones. A few fire-pits were considerably deeper, up to 55cm deep, and were possibly used to slow-roast larger foods at lower temperatures.

Cooking pot supports were also common, forty-six were found at Saar. These supports are an arrangement of upright plastered stones, usually three in number, used to hold a cooking pot. They are generally built alongside a wall, next to a hearth, and are about 20cm high. The supports could have been used to simmer a pot of food above a few embers – there is always ash around the supports and occasionally a thin layer of charcoal between them, or they could have been used to keep a pot of food warm after cooking.

Storage of food stuffs was obviously a primary concern for the Saar villagers and a large number of different storage facilities were found: sixty-seven plastered storage pits, twelve plastered single bins/basins, ten plastered double bins/basins, seven sunken storage jars and eleven storage vats. The storage pits were mainly round or oval and varied in size, ranging from 7cm to 62cm in depth, and up to 1m wide. They were lined with a hard, white, waterproof coating of plaster and so could have been used to store either solids or liquids. The bins or basins were both circular and square, and their waterproof plastered stonewalls could also have been used for either solids or liquids. The storage

Fig. 5.05
A buried storage jar, still sealed with a stone stopper. (Photo. courtesy of the Bahrain Ministry of Culture and Information).

jars and vats were sunk into the ground, their rims level with the floor, some still closed with stone or plaster stoppers (see **Fig.** 5.05).

The excavators suggested that the storage jars may have been used as household 'safes', keeping valuable items hidden from casual view, partly because there were so few of them and they were mostly found in the houses of wealthier families. Hidden in the corner of a dark room, sunk beneath the floor, they would only be visible to those actively seeking them. The pits, bins/basins and vats could have been used for storing grain - wheat and barley grains were found at Saar - dates or date products, for which there is plentiful evidence, or various liquids. Killick and Moon suggest the vats may even have been used for brewing beer (2005: 349).

The final built-in kitchen facilities found in the houses of Saar are benches with inset basins. Forty-four houses had these benches, usually set just inside the main door. They are rectangular structures built of stone and finished with a coat of plaster, typically just over a metre in length and about 60cm wide, one of the few intact examples measuring about 53cm high. The basins were set into the benches, taking up about a third of the top and being only a few centimetres deep. They were also finished with a coat of hard, white plaster. The bottom of the basins sloped, being deeper at the front, and a drainage lip was found on some of the better-preserved examples. One particularly well-preserved example has a central depression surrounded by a stone edge, which perhaps once held a container of water used for the washing of hands or utensils in the basin.

We have a very clear idea of the layout and facilities of an early Dilmun kitchen at Saar. We also have a great many cooking pots – over 60% of all the pottery recovered - utilitarian vessels with round bases, frequently showing signs of soot-blackening from use over cooking fires (see **Fig** 5.06). Other kitchenware includes an assortment of stone tools: grinders, pounders, mortars and choppers, used for grinding flour from cereals, and for processing vegetables, fruit and meats. Meals were probably eaten from a communal plate as diners gathered together around a palm-leaf mat.

Although archaeological evidence was only found for wheat, barley and dates, the villagers must have eaten a variety of agricultural produce. However, studies of teeth from Bahraini burials show that dental caries has been a common problem

throughout the centuries, including the early Dilmun period, something which is thought to be the result of the major role played by dates in the Bahraini diet (Nesbitt 1993: 37). It seems that the villagers of Saar may already have been eating a date-rich diet four thousand years ago.

There is plenty of evidence for fish and meat consumption at Saar. Sea fish bones dominate the faunal assemblage and so were clearly a major part of the diet (see **Fig.** 5.07). The fish species represented at Saar were very similar to the fish found in local markets today: emperors or *sha'ari* (Lethrinidae), groupers such as *hamour* (Serranidae), sea breams (Sparidae) and jack fish (Carangidae) were all favourites, fish which are caught close to the Bahrain coast (Uerpmann and Uerpmann 2003). A variety of fish hooks made from copper and bronze were found across the site (see **Fig.** 5.08), showing that the villagers were line fishing, but it is also possible that they used *haddrah*, fish traps, to catch many of these species which enter the intertidal zone at high tide. Interestingly, different households at Saar appeared to be eating different amounts and different types of fish, probably a reflection of different levels of wealth or status rather than of different tastes. There was little evidence for the consumption of marine mammals and, in contrast with other contemporary sites in the Gulf, little evidence for the consumption of turtles and cormorants. A considerable quantity of shellfish remains were found, though, including oysters, clams, scallops and cockles. The inhabitants of Saar were also hunters, catching and eating wild camel, sand gazelle and oryx using copper-headed spears and arrows.

The villagers kept a number of animals, for transport, for meat, and for products such as leather and bone. Donkeys were used for transporting people and goods - a picture of a donkey and rider

Fig. 5.06
A selection of the many pots found at Saar, these would have had a range of different functions. (Photo. courtesy of the Bahrain Ministry of Culture and Information).

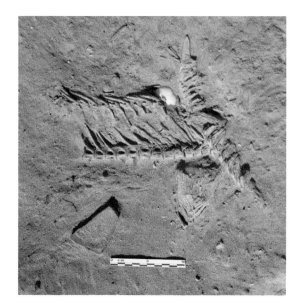

Fig. 5.07
The remains of a good dinner – bones of a grouper, big emperor and golden trevally. (Photo. courtesy of the Bahrain Ministry of Culture and Information).

Fig. 5.08
A copper fish hook, its corroded line still bound around the top. (Photo. courtesy of the Bahrain Ministry of Culture and Information).

Fig. 5.09
The seal found at Saar
showing a donkey
being ridden. (Photo.
courtesy of the Bahrain
Ministry of Culture and
Information).

was engraved on one of the seals found at Saar (see **Fig.** 5.09). Sheep, goats and a small number of cattle were kept principally for food. In addition, sheep could have supplied wool and goats could have supplied hair for textiles and possibly also milk. Interestingly, most of the sheep kept at Saar were a local breed, and much smaller than those kept at the contemporary city at Qala'at al-Bahrain which were similar to Mesopotamian breeds.

During the years the village was occupied fish and animal bone fragments had been steadily discarded across the site, swept into the yards and against the walls inside the rooms. Several of these bones had also been gnawed by rats and the bones of black rats were also found across the site, showing that the Saar villagers had suffered from these pests. Margarethe and Hans-Peter Uerpmann, the faunal specialists, suggest that the villagers may have introduced the grey mongoose in an attempt to control their rat problem (2005: 307).

Fig. 5.10
Seal showing two men
wearing tiered skirts
and hats. (Photo.
courtesy of the Bahrain
Ministry of Culture and
Information).

Fig. 5.11
The teeth of a bone
comb, the longest is
2.5cm long. (Photo.
courtesy of the Bahrain
Ministry of Culture and
Information).

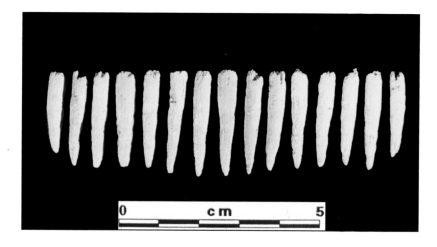

Although no clothing from the Early Dilmun period survives, we do have clay-impressions of cloth, and pictures of people on seals give us some idea of the dress of the Saar villagers (see **Fig** 5.10). Sixteen bone teeth that must have been broken from a comb tell us that neat hairstyles were important (see **Fig.** 5.11). We also have a range of jewellery, including copper finger-rings and bangle, rings of shell and bone, and beads made from copper, clay, glass, faience, local and imported shell, and a variety of stones, including imported, exotic carnelian (see **Fig.** 5.12 and **Fig.** 5.13). Fourteen small pearls were found at Saar, though none of them was pierced for stringing so we cannot be sure how they were actually used.

A number of other artefacts tell us yet more about the daily lives of the Saar community. For example, there is some evidence that their lives were not all hard work. Two small clay cones and caches of pebbles are thought to be gaming pieces, there are fragments of bird-bone whistles and flutes, and pictures on seals found at Saar show scenes of dancing and feasting (see **Fig.** 5.14). More enigmatic objects are the five crude animal figurines made from baked clay that were found at Saar. Similar figurines are found throughout the Middle East and date from many periods, but their original meaning or purpose remains unclear. They may have been children's toys, they may have had some ritual significance, or they may be something else entirely.

It is possible that the inhabitants of Saar were involved in some direct trading. There are weights from two international standards: a chert cube Indus weight of the Dilmun standard (see **Fig.** 5.15), and a tapered cylinder of black, polished stone of Babylonian type which fits the Ur standard. These weights suggest the villagers were not just trading with their local Bahraini neighbours, but needed to

Fig. 5.12 A bone ring, 2.8cm in width. (Photo. courtesy of the Bahrain Ministry of Culture and Information).

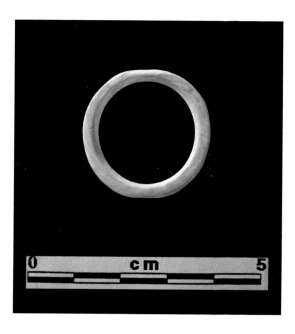

Fig. 5.13
A group of clay beads found on the floor of one of the houses (restrung). Clay was the most common material used for beads at Saar, probably as it was the least expensive. The largest bead is 6mm in length. (Photo. courtesy of the Bahrain Ministry of Culture and Information).

Fig. 5.14
Scenes of people
drinking together, on
a seal found at Saar.
(Photo. courtesy of
the Bahrain Ministry
of Culture and
Information).

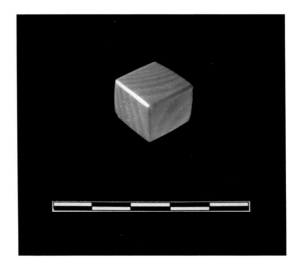

Fig. 5.15
Cubic stone weight
of Indus Valley type
conforming to the
Dilmun standard.
(Photo. courtesy of
the Bahrain Ministry
of Culture and
Information).

Fig. 5.16
A copper awl, used for
piercing holes in wood
or leather, still in its
bone handle. (Photo.
courtesy of the Bahrain
Ministry of Culture and
Information).

Fig. 5.16
A copper awl, used for piercing holes in wood or leather, still in its bone handle. (Photo. courtesy of the Bahrain Ministry of Culture and Information).

check the weights of more exotic commodities sold by more specialised merchants. Certainly several imported materials were found at the site: bitumen from Iran, stone and shell from the Arabian mainland, copper probably from Oman (see **Fig. 5.16**), carnelian from the Indus valley, lapis lazuli from Afghanistan, elephant ivory probably from East Africa, and pottery from Mesopotamia, the Indus valley and southeast Arabia.

The Temple

At the highest point of the village, at the main crossroads of the settlement, sits the temple (see **Fig. 5.17**). The building is unique, not only different from the village houses that surround it, but also with no known parallels from other Dilmun period sites. It is an irregular trapezoid shape with a curious bulge in the external wall at the western corner (see **Fig. 5.18**). The excavators suggested this shape was dictated by the existing street pattern, and that the temple was sandwiched awkwardly between the adjacent houses at this focal point of

Fig. 5.17
An aerial view of the temple, which stands at the centre of the village. (Photo. courtesy of the Bahrain Ministry of Culture and Information).

the settlement. It was first built during the second phase of occupation at the site (c. 2000-1950 BC), but was extensively remodelled during the third phase about a century later when most of the village was rebuilt. The walls were built of local stone and were originally heavily plastered both inside and out and, rising above the surrounding landscape, the village temple would have been visible for miles around.

The building interior is not large, and could only have held a small number of people at any one time, either the priests alone or select groups of worshippers. It would have been a dark, restricted space. There was only one entrance in the eastern corner and no evidence for any windows. We know

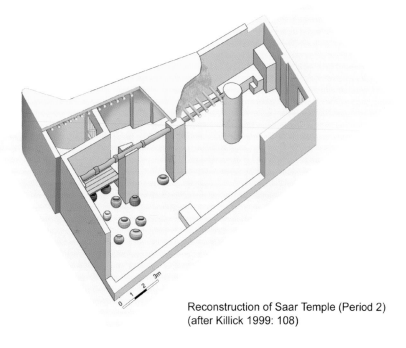

Reconstruction of Saar Temple (Period 2)
(after Killick 1999: 108)

Fig. 5.18
A reconstruction drawing of the Saar temple.

it was originally roofed - the two large square columns and one round column which run down the centre of the building supported a roof made from wooden beams covered with palm fronds and sealed with mud or plaster. We also know from fragments of wall plaster that at least some of the interior was originally painted crimson. A model of the Saar temple can be seen in the National Museum.

There were three areas of the temple that seem to have been the focus of cult activities: a group of stone benches in the northern corner, a central altar and an altar on the southeastern wall. A high bench approached by two low steps was built to the right of the entrance way during the construction of the temple, and continued in use throughout its life, both the bench and steps being replastered several times. In fact the high bench is the only feature in the temple that was never altered, suggesting that either the altar, or whatever was placed upon it, was of great significance. Two lower benches, a short and a long one, were originally built along the northwestern wall, though after the temple was remodelled these were replaced by a single bench and a raised floor level reduced the height of the high bench by half. At this time a square plinth was added to the southern end of the high bench, 15 cm higher than the bench. The area around the benches appears to have received preferential treatment, the floor was kept very clean and some surfaces may have been covered with matting. Indentations in the plaster on top of these benches indicated that objects with rectangular bases had been placed upon them. Killick and Moon suggested that these objects may have been statues of gods in human form and cultic symbols. This was certainly the practice in the cities of southern Babylon, an area with which Dilmun shared a degree of religious iconography and practices.

There are now two altars in the temple, but originally it had only one, that on the southeastern wall. The central altar was added during the major rebuild of phase three, at which time the southern altar was also remodelled. This was partly necessitated by the new, higher floor level, but a crescent-shaped altar back was also added. The central altar had a similar shaped back and was built facing in the same direction and on roughly the same alignment as the southern altar.

Crawford, Killick and Moon suggest that these crescent shaped altars reflect the worship of a moon god at the Saar temple (1997: 91). They show that scenes of men worshipping before crescent symbols are relatively common on Dilmun seals, often with a second symbol thought to be a 'sunburst'. In Babylonian religion these symbols represent the sun and the moon, and they argue that the strong connections between Babylonian and Dilmunite practices would support a similar interpretation here; the Saar crescent-shaped altars represent the crescent moon. They also mention the connection between the crescent horns of the Babylonian moon god Sin and cattle, and suggest it may be possible such a connection also existed at Saar.

There is archaeological evidence for use of the altars. Microstratigraphical and micromorphological analyses of some areas of the temple were conducted by The McDonald Institute for Archaeological Research at the University of Cambridge. This was the first time such a study, which examines the floor sequences and occupation debris in minute detail, had been conducted in the Gulf. Ash found on top of both altars and dumped beside them showed that they were used for ritual burning, and variations in the concentration suggest that the intensity of ceremonial activities varied over time. Most of the ash came from date-palms, though it also contained tiny fragments of bone suggesting that burnt offerings were made on the altars. The archaeologists also looked for evidence of the burning of incense, a common practice throughout the Near East at this time. Organic staining was found in many of the deposits on top of the altars, and samples are being tested for evidence of frankincense.

It is thought the western end of the temple was used as a storage area. A small room was built into the western corner, where the bulge occurs in the exterior wall. In the plaster floor of this room were depressions for storage jars, and sherds from large jars and pieces of bitumen were found in the deposit. A series of door sockets show that the room had a door. Killick and Moon suggest that some of the broken sealings found in this area may have been door sealings from the room, which may have been kept for storing valuable ritual items and materials. Less valuable items may have been stored outside the room. There were more depressions in the floor across the southwestern end of the temple, where microstratigraphy and micromorphology showed that these floors were relatively dirty and swept infrequently, and a number of broken seal impressions showed that boxes and pottery storage jars had once been opened here.

In front of the temple entrance was a public space. Two stone altars or offering tables stood in this space, being increased to five in the final phase of the temple's use. There is no evidence for any burnt offerings on or around these altars, and no sign of scorching on the stone itself, so they clearly played a role different from that of the interior altars. Killick and Moon suggest they may have been used to receive the private donations or offerings of individuals, or, alternatively, for the public display of statues or cult symbols.

We can picture this small temple at the centre of village life, standing at the highest point of the ridge, its thick, plastered walls visible above the small terraced houses which cluster around it. The interior of the temple is dark and hidden, and the priests hide their religious paraphernalia, locked away from prying eyes, at the very back of the building. Villagers gather in the open space outside, perhaps to gaze upon statues of their gods or to offer small personal donations. Small groups of them may enter to worship, perhaps to witness the ritual burning of their offerings on the altars of the moon god, the smell of burnt flesh mingling with that of incense. Finally, we have a direct glimpse of some of these worshippers from long ago. In patches of plaster floor dating from the second phase of the temple's use were found two sets of footprints, those of an adult by the stone benches and central column, and, by the circular column, those of a child.

The Burial Grounds

Not only can we see where and how the Saar villagers lived four thousand years ago, we also know what happened to them when they came to the end of their lives. West of the village was one of the great Dilmun mound fields, perhaps comprising 15,000 mounds. Most of these mounds are now gone, cleared to allow the construction of the causeway to Saudi Arabia, but teams led by Dr. Moawiyah Ibrahim and Dr. Mohammad Mughal, and more recently a team from the Bahraini Directorate of Antiquities, were able to excavate a great many before their inevitable destruction. These mounds follow the general design common across Bahrain, a rectangular stone-built chamber sealed with a large stone or stones and surrounded by a ring wall, though some mounds contained more chambers or had had further ring-walls and graves added. As mentioned in Chapter Four the London-Bahrain Archaeological Expedition rebuilt a burial with four shaft graves at the Saar site and this gives a very good idea of how the graves would originally have appeared.

South of the village lies a second, contemporary graveyard, the Southern Burial Complex or 'Honeycomb Cemetery', which was also excavated by the Arab team led by Drs. Ibrahim and Mughal. This cemetery was different in style from the mound fields, and as its name suggests the graves here were built next to each other, radiating out from the central grave rather like the cells of a honeycomb. A further group of 'honeycomb' type graves was found to the north of this cemetery - possibly an extension of the main Southern Burial Complex – and along the eastern edge of these graves was an area reserved for the burial of children.

Fig. 5.19
The design on the
seal found in a
grave in the Saar
cemetery. Fragments
of impressed sealings
made with this
seal were found in
Building 207. (Photo.
courtesy of the Bahrain
Ministry of Culture and
Information).

Dr. Bruno Frohlich, an anthropologist at the Smithsonian Institution, analysed the remains of 92 skeletons found in the burial mounds and honeycomb graves at Saar (Frohlich 1982). Of these 14 could be identified as adult males, 15 as adult females, 23 as adults of indeterminate sex, and 10 as children. Poor preservation conditions meant that the bones of children and infants were less likely to survive, so they are under represented in the archaeological record. Dr. Frohlich calculated the average height of the Saar villagers based upon measurements of the longbones found. Interestingly he found that, compared to other contemporary populations in the Near East, the Bahrainis were relatively tall. Men here were on average 171cm and women 166cm, whereas at Bab edh-Dhra in Jordan for example, men were on average 165cm and women 155cm tall. He also suggested that several villagers may have lived to a respectable old age as their bones showed that they had suffered from degenerative arthritis.

The graves had largely been robbed in antiquity but a variety of grave goods still remained, mainly pottery and seals. One particularly interesting seal was found by the Bahraini team in one of the graves in the moundfield (Al-Sindi 1999: 218). This seal shows what Killick and Moon describe as "almost a pictorial summary of life in Dilmun" (2005: 348), a man surrounded by a gazelle, birds, a net and a shield or hide (see **Fig.** 5.19). A group of sealing fragments found in Building 207 in the village were made using this very same seal. Through the discovery of the seal we can see the life and death of one particular Saar villager – the remains of goods sealed as part of daily business transactions, and the final grave and resting place.

Chapter Six

Al-Khamis Mosque and Bilad al-Qadim

The white minarets of the Al-Khamis mosque hold a special place in the hearts of Bahrainis. It is the oldest mosque found on the islands and, according to local tradition, dates originally from the early eighth century AD. The structure that stands today, however, is the result of several phases of rebuilding, with the columns and arches being added in the tenth century and a second minaret in the fourteenth. Only the Qiblah niche survives from the earliest building. Although the mosque now stands next to the busy Shaikh Salman Highway surrounded by modern development, it is possible to gain some idea of its past and the lives of those who worshipped here. The surrounding area is known as Bilad al-Qadim, which translates as "The Old Town" or "The Old Country", and recent archaeological research and local history give us a rich picture of Bahrain's first Islamic communities (see **Fig.** 6.01).

Directions to Site

The Al-Khamis Mosque is next to the Sheikh Salman Highway, opposite the Khamis Police Station. Turn off the highway onto one of the side roads, where there is limited parking available outside the mosque. The site is open on Sunday-Wednesday from 7am-2pm, on Thursday and Saturday from 9am-6pm, and on Friday from 3pm-6pm. Entry to the mosque is free. There are plans underway to build a small site museum, which will display some of the more interesting artefacts found

at the site. The Al-Hassan Mosque mound is on the opposite side of the Highway. At present it is fenced in to protect the site, but will be open to the public once the Al-Khamis museum is completed. The Abu Zaydan spring is also closed at present, but it too will be open after the construction of the museum.

Past Research

The area surrounding the Al-Khamis mosque has changed enormously in the past forty years. Early photographs and accounts of European visitors show us the scale of change. Mr and Mrs Theodore Bent, who visited Bahrain in 1889, write of the "interesting ruins" of the "ancient capital", and describe how the "minarets and pillars of the old mosques looked down on a strange scene that day. In the half-ruined, domed houses of the departed race, stall-holders had pitched their stalls: lanes and cross lanes of closely-packed vendors" (Rice 1984: 101-2). This market, held each week on a Thursday, gave its name to the mosque, "Al-Khamis", or "Thursday", and it is still sometimes called the Suq Al-Khamis, or "Thursday Market", Mosque. Mackay, writing in 1925, describes how, "a village, once very prosperous, but now entirely deserted, is Bilad el Qadim" and also mentions some low mounds of "late date" and large tumuli which had been "rifled" (Rice 1984:159).

Although Mackay's description of mounds and tumuli suggest that the remains of past settlement could be found in Bilad al-Qadim, most archaeological work has been concentrated at the Al-Khamis Mosque. Today, new development covers most of the surrounding area and only a few small places remain as clues to the first town. A team from Manchester University, led by Prof. Timothy Insoll and working with the Bahrain National Museum were lucky enough to investigate these few remaining mounds in 2001.

Fig. 6.01
Excavations in progress at the Al-Khamis mosque in 2001, the famous white minarets in the background. (Photo. Insoll and MacLean).

The mosque, however, has been protected, and has been excavated on several occasions (see **Fig.** 6.02). In 1950 the Bahrain Government rescued the decaying building, re-erecting the blocks and columns that had fallen and clearing back the scrub that at that time surrounded the site. They found two teak pillars over 4m in height, supporting a horizontal beam upon which the ceiling rested, which were removed during the renovations. Teak is an exotic wood that would have been imported, most probably from India, and reflects the large sum of money spent on this construction phase of the mosque. Diez, who visited the mosque in the early part of the twentieth century, observed a stone with a long inscription in the Qibla wall of the courtyard that gave a fourteenth century date for the most recent phase of building. This stone had fallen by 1950 and is now on display in the National Museum. A French team under the direction of Monik Kervran carried out extensive excavations of the mosque in the 1980s, confirming the dating of the various phases of the building (Kervran 1990). The publication of their work is still eagerly awaited.

Most recently Prof. Insoll's team opened several small units in various parts of the mosque precinct (see **Fig.** 6.01). These excavations, together with the excavation of a large mound on the opposite side of the highway, produced evidence of settlement dating from the eighth century AD, the time of the building of the mosque according to local tradition (see **Fig.** 6.03). Excitingly, other local stories were also echoed by the archaeological evidence, which showed a history of occupation from the eighth to the fourteenth century. These excavations told of ordinary daily lives, the baking of bread and worship in the local mosque; but also a tale of merchants dealing in exotic products, soldiers housed within the thick walls of a fort, and the poisoning of the local well by a man angry at his lack of success in finding a wife in Bilad al-Qadim.

Fig. 6.02 (opposite) A plan of the Al-Khamis mosque.

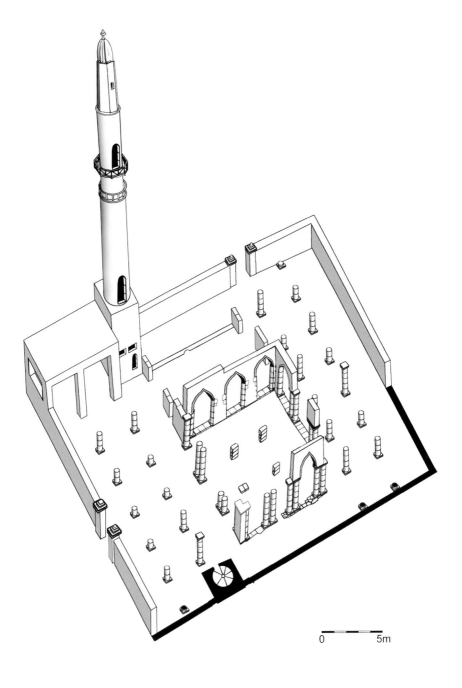

Axonometric reconstruction of the Al-Khamis Mosque
(after Kervran1990: 30)

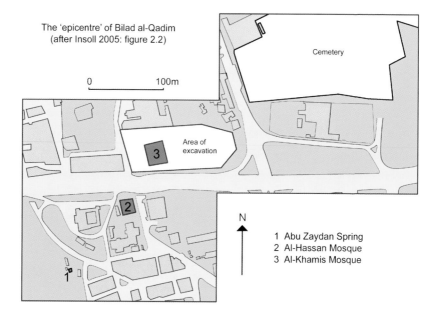

Fig. 6.03
The centre of Bilad al-Qadim showing Professor Insoll's 2001 excavation units.

The Site Today

The most distinctive features of the Al-Khamis mosque are its two minarets and these are normally open to brave and agile visitors. Certainly the views from the small windows are worth the climb – though please take care as the steps are uneven and narrow. The old ablutions area of the mosque can also be seen to the left of the building as you enter, at the bottom of a narrow trench. The main area excavated by Professor Insoll and his team has been left open and is at the far side of the site. During the construction of the site museum this area will be conserved and presented to the public in a more informative way. Similarly, when the Al-Hassan Mosque site and Abu Zaydan spring are re-opened, they too will be clearly signed with new information boards.

The Story from Archaeology

The Al-Khamis Mosque and Market

Although today visitors to the Al-Khamis site come to gaze upon Bahrain's oldest standing mosque, the work of Prof. Insoll's team revealed that, in the past, other buildings stood in its shadow. Geophysical survey of the site showed many areas where walls once rose; the mosque had in fact stood in a densely occupied urban environment, crammed with many small buildings. The scatter of archaeological material across the surface attested to the intensive use of this space in the past. Part of this area had then become a cemetery, some of the grave markers from which are still displayed beside the mosque, having been moved from their original position in recent years.

The Manchester team followed up the geophysical survey with a series of excavations, taking care to avoid the areas that appeared to contain graves.

Fig. 6.04
A traditional *tannur* oven in use on Bahrain in 2010. (Photo. Insoll and MacLean).

Work was always halted if any signs of past burials were found. To the northwest of the mosque excavations revealed part of a kitchen that was found to date from the mid-eleventh to twelfth century AD. The top of a traditional round clay oven, a *tannur*, was uncovered, similar to the ovens still used in Bahrain today to bake the flat bread, *khubz* (see **Fig.** 6.04). Inside the oven the contents had clearly once been organic. This oven was set in a white plaster floor, and half a grinding stone, used for grinding grain into flour, was found lying nearby.

To the east of the mosque a much larger area was excavated, and here the remains of an alleyway once lined with small buildings was found (see **Fig.** 6.05). Several different phases of use and rebuilding were identified, dating from the eighth to the fourteenth century AD. Below the structures ran an earlier rock-cut channel that would originally have been used for irrigation, though later, particularly during the eleventh to thirteenth centuries, it was used for disposing of rubbish. The small buildings opening on to the alleyway are reminiscent of the traditional shops of a Bahraini souk, small units with raised floors in which traders would haggle over the price of goods with their customers and artisans would spend their days manufacturing such items as brass coffee pots and leather shoes. The archaeological evidence suggests that these buildings may have been used for a range of activities: housing, workshops, retail units and storage space.

That food was stored in the buildings was suggested by the large amount of broken bone from the tiny rodents and insectivores that tend to prey upon domestic stores. Food storage may also have been the purpose of a complete pot with a stone lid that was found embedded within a section of wall. There was other evidence for food preparation and consumption. A variety of animal bones clearly

Fig. 6.05 (pages 132-133)
The row of small buildings found next to the Al-Khamis mosque. (Photo. Insoll and MacLean).

showed signs of butchery - beef, mutton, goat and camel were all part of the diet of this community. There was also extensive evidence for chicken, fish and shellfish consumption. Bones from some of the larger fish, species such as shark, rays and groupers, showed cut marks that suggested the fish had been processed on the site, either for immediate domestic consumption or for splitting prior to salting. Larger fish are still treated this way today, being split, rubbed with rock salt and dried in the sun, before being stored, salted, in barrels or bowls. Dried fish is today sold primarily to travellers: pilgrims, those on hunting trips and "people living in the wilderness" (Abass 2002: 35-36). Could these fish bones be the remains of a past local trade in dried fish?

Other less common species were also represented in the archaeology. There were a number of cormorant bones which appeared to have been roasted and butchered; although not eaten on Bahrain today, cormorant was on the menu in the Hawar islands until relatively recently (Ian Smith 2005: 201). There were also some turtle bones that showed signs of cooking, and a few fragments of dolphin teeth. Samuel Miles, a Political Agent and Consul based in Muscat in the late nineteenth century, described dolphin as "good eating" (1919: 407), though he thought shark a more important part of the Gulf diet.

A more unexpected find was a pig bone with a number of cuts marks made during butchery. Pork is not normally found in the diet of an orthodox Muslim, and the presence of this bone in the diet waste of Bilad al-Qadim therefore suggests a more complex picture. It is possible that this pig bone reflects a community that was mixed in character, with those of other faiths living peacefully alongside the Muslim majority, much as they do today.

A second clay oven was also found in this area, again containing a carbonized organic material. This oven was later in date, being built and used in the twelfth or thirteenth century. Whilst ovens may be found in individual houses, community bakeries continue to be common in the more traditional areas of Bahrain, and thus this oven may be either evidence of a single household or of the presence of such a bakery in the midst of the souk. Plant remains do not survive well on Bahrain unless they have been charred or burnt, so in general archaeologists have little evidence for this part of the diet. However, from these excavations of the market area we do have the charred remains of both barley and wheat, cereal crops that could have been ground to provide the flour used in the bread ovens.

Other areas of these buildings produced evidence for craftworking. A concentration of metalworking debris, including grinders and slag, represented at least two separate episodes of iron smelting (the production of iron from iron ore). There was also evidence of lead casting, probably the activities of small-scale artisan craft workers. A purple residue thickly encrusting several fragments of a white earthenware vessel dating from the eleventh century was interpreted as a purple dye. *Hexaplex* shells, which were found in some numbers on the site, can be boiled to make a similar purple dye. These pot sherds may, therefore, represent either the production of this dye at the site, or the work of a cloth dyer. We know cloth was being produced locally because several spindle whorls, used by women to spin thread from cotton or flax, were also found.

Finally, there was evidence for the more exotic trades of the souk merchants (see **Fig.** 6.06), and in particular for the commodity for which Bahrain has been famous for centuries, pearls. Two pearls, both perforated for stringing, were found, one dating from the eleventh century and one from the late twelfth or thirteenth century (see **Fig.**

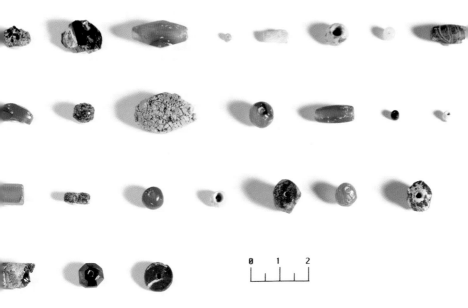

Fig. 6.06
A selection of beads, some of imported materials, found in excavations in Bilad al-Qadim. (Photo. Insoll and MacLean).

Fig. 6.07
The two pearls found in the Al-Khamis souk, drilled for stringing. (Photo. Insoll and MacLean).

6.07). In the same group of buildings a fragment of a pierced copper sheet was found, which closely resembles the sieves used by Bahrain's dealers to grade their pearls. To grade the pearls according to size, they were passed through a series of brass or copper bowls, *tasah*, which fitted one inside each other, and the pearls would then be divided into four groups according to size, from the largest, *ras*, through *batn*, *dhayl*, to the smallest, *sahtit*. The pearls were weighed using a measuring system known as *khows*. Their final value was determined from several factors, not only size, but also shape, colour and beauty, and deals were conducted using a secret, silent code to preserve privacy.

The great wealth that pearls brought was also represented archaeologically. A number of coins and metal weights or tokens were found at the Al-Khamis site, but notable amongst them were three

Fig. 6.08
One of the three gold dinars found at the Al-Khamis site. This is a coin attributed to the Fatimid Caliph Nezar al-Aziz, dated 379 AH (AD 989) and minted at Mansuriya near Kairouan, Tunisia. (Photo. Insoll and MacLean).

gold dinars (see **Fig.** 6.08). The inscriptions on these coins tell us when they were minted, although they could, and did, remain in use for many years. They date originally from AD 750-751, AD 786-809 and AD 989, with the later coin being minted in Kairouan, Tunisia. In addition to these gold coins, seven copper coins and thirty lead coins or weights were found. None of these bore any datable inscriptions. There are historical accounts of lead coinage being used elsewhere in the region; Nasir-i-Khusraw, an eleventh century Persian poet and traveller, describes the use of sacks or baskets of lead for transactions, and some of the lead coins at the Al-Khamis were found in an eleventh century context. A more unusual use for these lead tokens is suggested by an intriguing story associated with the Al-Hassan site that lies a few metres to the southwest of the Al-Khamis and which is discussed below.

The Al-Hassan Mosque, Palace and Fort

Lying on the opposite side of the Shaikh Salman Highway from the Al-Khamis Mosque is a small mound which, when excavated by Prof. Insoll and his team (see **Fig.** 6.09), revealed a long history

Fig. 6.09
Excavations in progress
at the Al-Hassan
mound, 2001. (Photo.
Insoll and MacLean).

of use. Most recently it was topped by a mosque, known locally as the Al-Hassan or Haroun mosque, and a shrine. Neither the mosque nor the shrine had been used within living memory, and the building had been flattened, but it remains a site of historical importance to the local community.

According to one story told today the mosque was named after Haroun, a man who came to Bilad al-Qadim to find a wife. Being unsuccessful, in his anger he filled an adjacent well with lead weights to poison the water supply and cause the water to dry up. A similar story was recorded in the nineteenth century by Durand (1879: 1):

"in the time of Merwan, a Chief called Ibn Hakim came from Katif wishing to marry a lovely daughter of the Bahrain Chief. Titles, or money, must, however, have been wanting, as the story goes that his operations were treated with contempt. On this he began warlike operations by depriving the thirsty

Bahrainees of their accustomed drink. He seized three wells, one at Ali, one in the Bilad-i-Kadim, and one close to Bahrain called Daraz. When these were filled in, the guardian deity of the island was good enough to make them break out in the places still marked by the springs opposite to Muharrak. The invader was eventually defeated and retired to the mainland."

Coins which have been dated to 684 AD bear the name of the Caliph Merwan, and the coins of Merwan II have been dated to 744-750 AD, giving a rough date to the story. However, there is no known connection between these coins and the site. There were many lead items discovered in the excavations at the neighbouring Al-Khamis site, however, and it is entirely possible that they could be the "lead weights" referred to in the story, and therefore evidence that the poisoning of the water was an actual historical event (see **Fig.** 6.10).

Fig. 6.10
Lead 'coins' or 'weights' found in the excavations at Al-Khamis. Are these the lead weights once used to poison the drinking water of Bilad al-Qadim, as told in local legend? (Photo. Insoll and MacLean).

Beneath the more recent mosque was a long sequence of buildings, the very earliest being a water channel cut into the bedrock. It was not possible to date the cutting of this channel, which would have been used to irrigate land and carry clean drinking water. Above the channel had been built a structure that appears to have been a small fort. Its thick, high walls built of stone and plaster certainly suggest a defensive purpose, though its small size would be more typical of a guardhouse or even a single fortified house. A steep plaster staircase runs up an internal wall and four circular indentations set in the plaster floor may have been used for the storage of water jars (see **Fig.** 6.11). Interestingly, Belgrave, writing in 1973, records that, "According to local reports the sandy mound near the School opposite Suq al-Khamis Mosque is all that remains of the fort that protected the town" (1973: 148).

A range of pot sherds was found in the deposits associated with the fort, mainly from locally produced ceramics but including some imported wares, most notably a piece of Chinese White Ware. These enabled the fort to be dated to the eighth or early ninth centuries AD. There was also evidence of ironworking in the fort, and blacksmithing in particular; an area of burnt rubble and pieces of crucibles and iron slag were found.

In the ninth or early tenth century AD the fort was remodelled and new building-work took place. This new building had good quality plaster floors and coloured plaster decorated the walls; it has been interpreted as a rich merchant's house, or even part of a palace. The height of the surviving walls suggest it may have been at least two storeys high. In the mud plaster of the walls the impressions of the builders' fingers could be clearly seen, giving us a direct link to the Bahrainis of a millennium ago. In the floor plaster a pot sherd on which is written the beginning of the *basmalah* was found,

suggesting that this was the home of a Muslim community. This building was occupied for many years and new floors were laid over time. Again, a range of pot sherds were found, including those from imported vessels, but there is also a great deal of evidence for pottery production on the site; kiln wasters (vessels which went wrong during the firing process) and three-cornered kiln tripods or trivets used to separate vessels in the kiln (see **Fig. 6.12**). Most of this evidence dates from the twelfth and thirteenth centuries. Indeed, there is so much evidence for pottery manufacture on the site that it has been suggested that Bahrain could even have been exporting pottery to other parts of the region.

Some of the most interesting archaeological evidence from the house were the animal and fish bones which tell us about the diet of the time. The variety of animals eaten contrasts with other periods, and included, in addition to the more common goat, sheep, cattle and chicken: cormorant, hare, camel, dog and turtle. The dog is prohibited meat for a Muslim. The bones found on this site showed clear signs of butchery, which, like the pig bones found at the Al-Khamis site, suggests that the community living at Bilad al-Qadim in the late twelfth and thirteenth century was not wholly an orthodox Islamic one. Those of other faiths may have been living alongside their Muslim neighbours, Christians for example are able to eat dog meat.

Fig. 6.11
The stairs inside the fort. Below them is the deep water channel, and beside them the circular indentations in the floor that may have been used for storing water jars. (Photo. Insoll and MacLean).

Amongst these twelfth and thirteenth century deposits were also an unusually large number of cat bones, several of which display cut marks that strongly suggest that the animals had been skinned. There is no historical record of the use of cat fur or skin on Bahrain, or of the eating of cat meat. It is hard, therefore, to know why cats were being routinely skinned at this date. It is also very difficult to identify the species of cat represented, though

Fig. 6.12 These trivets were used to separate pots in the kiln during firing. (Photo. Insoll and MacLean).

Ian Smith, the faunal specialist who worked on the material, concluded that they were either wild cats (*Felis silvestris*), domestic cats (*Felis catus*) or a hybrid of the two (2005: 205-6). It is interesting that these cat remains were disposed of in the same area as the potters' waste – was there some connection?

The palatial house finally fell into disuse, to be replaced by a mosque in the thirteenth or fourteenth century AD. The mosque reused some of the existing walls of the house, and was built upon the mound that had formed over the centuries of remodelling.

Excavations revealed various floors laid over time, of both plaster and shell, and the remains of arches that had eventually fallen. The mosque continued in use until the eighteenth or nineteenth century – a small copper coin of this date was found in the uppermost floor.

Abu Zaydan Spring and Mosque

Today it is not really possible to visit the site of Abu Zaydan without a local guide. What was once a "most beautiful mosque" (Lewcock 1986: 493) built over a freshwater spring and bathing pool is now largely derelict and overgrown, and is a dangerous place for the unwary to explore (see **Fig.** 6.13). The spring would almost certainly have supplied the Early Islamic communities of Bilad al-Qadim – Al-Idrisi, writing in the mid-twelfth century, talks of the Abu Zaydan spring in his book *Nuzhat al-Mushtaq*.

Fig. 6.13
The site of Abu Zaydan, having been cleaned prior to restoration in 2010. (Photo. Insoll and MacLean).

Fig. 6.14
The pillar supporting the Abu Zaydan mosque, made reusing stone drums from an older building. (Photo. Insoll and MacLean).

The pool we see today was re-modelled and re-tiled in the twentieth century, but elements used in the structure are much older. Providing support for a central pillar holding up the floor of the overhead mosque are four stone drums (see **Fig.** 6.14). The second drum from the top has a carved channel and spout (see **Fig** 6.15) and would appear to be an up-turned altar or libations table – the channel would have allowed blood and sacrificial liquids to flow from the altar. Similar altar stones have been found at the Dilmun period Barbar Temple dating from about 2,000 BC. The use of these stones in the Abu Zaydan pool suggests that a Dilmun period temple once stood in Bilad al-Qadim. Further evidence of a Dilmun settlement was found by Captain Edward Durand in the nineteenth century (1880: 193). He bought an inscribed stone of black basalt from a mosque, the Madrassah-i-Daood (now destroyed), in Bilad al-Qadim, and the Akkadian dialect of the inscription allowed it to be dated to

Fig. 6.15
The stone drum with a carved channel and spout, possibly a re-used Dilmun period altar stone. (Photo. Insoll and MacLean).

the Kassite period, the mid/late second millennium BC. Although this stone is presumed to have been destroyed during World War II, a replica is on display in the Bahrain National Museum.

It is particularly interesting that something as important as an altar stone was incorporated into the support for the mosque. Could this reflect the extreme importance of the well and bathing pool to the community living in Bilad al-Qadim? Could it also reflect some sort of symbolic continuity in the importance of water? The sacred well at Barbar has been described as "the unique entrance to the Absu", the Absu being the "Abyss of still, subterranean water" (Rice n.d.: 16), and there appears to be a clear link between the location of springs and Dilmun temples. Water also plays an important role in Islam, in Paradise imagery for example. It is possible that the first mosques in Bahrain were also built at the sites of springs and wells, and that the

Abu Zaydan mosque was deliberately built above the Abu Zaydan spring continuing a long-held association of spirituality with water.

In 2001 the pool was cleared of undergrowth and the deposits within it carefully excavated. In the earlier dark silt layer around the spring mouth only a handful of water-worn pottery sherds were found, and as the spring and bathing pool would have been kept clean when in use this was only to be expected.

Chapter Seven

The Tree of Life

The Tree of Life has long been one of Bahrain's best-known natural sites, and was even nominated as one of the New Seven Wonders of Nature in 2009. It has a mythical status in Bahrain, an enormous tree growing alone in the desert with no sign of water for miles around, with local stories claiming the tree could be 4,000 years old. It is probably a mesquite tree (*Prosopis cineraria*) and in reality is about 400 years old, still a considerable age for a mesquite which normally live for around 150 years. It grows on top of a small mound that is actually an archaeological site.

Walking over the mound it is possible, if you look carefully, to see the lines of walls in the sand. These are made from blocks of coral and traces of mortar are also visible. There is a scatter of archaeological material across the area, particularly on the right of the mound as you look at it from the approach road. Pieces of broken ceramics, fragments of glass, beads and small pieces of metal have all been found here, all material which suggests a date of the sixteenth century AD and later.

Bahraini archaeologists began excavations in 2010 (see **Fig.** 7.01) and these are starting to provide more definite information on the nature of the site and its date. They have now uncovered numerous small rooms built with large mud and stone walls, suggesting a village once stood here. Large, complete, green and blue glazed pots were found in several of these rooms. It appears that fish formed an important part of the Bahraini diet even here in the desert as large quantities of fish bones have been

Fig. 7.01
Excavations at the Tree
of Life, 2010. (Photo.
Insoll and MacLean).

found, some of considerable size. A radiocarbon date obtained from these excavations gives a date range of 1440-1640 AD. The freshwater well that must once have sustained this desert village is probably the secret of the Tree of Life's long success.

Directions to Site

The Tree of Life is in the desert, south-east of Jebel Dukhan. It is signed from the Al Muaskar Highway, but the signs are few and far between and there are few landmarks and several roads through the desert. Drive past the Riffa Golf Club (follow the signs for Riffa Views) and turn right at the roundabout, continue to go straight on unless signed otherwise. The Tree of Life lies to the right of the road, the only large tree visible in the desert.

References

Abass, M. 2002. Drying Fish in Bahrain. *Al-Ma'thurat Al-Sha'biyyah* 65: 33-36.

Al-Sindi, K.M. 1999. *Dilmun Seals*. Bahrain: Ministry of Cabinet Affairs and Information.

Andersen, H.H. and Højlund, F. 2003. *The Barbar Temples*. Moesgaard: Jutland Archaeological Society.

André-Salvini, B. 1999. The Cuneiform Tablets of Qala'at al-Bahrain. In *Bahrain The Civilisation of the Two Seas. From Dilmun to Tylos* (exhibition catalogue). Paris: Institut du Monde, pp. 126-129.

Audioguide Tour. Qala'at al-Bahrain. (Leaflet). Bahrain; Ministry of Culture and Information.

Bangsgaard, P. 2003. Animal Bones. In *The Barbar Temples*. Volume 2. Appendices. Moesgaard: Jutland Archaeological Society, pp. 7-16.

Belgrave, J. 1973. *Welcome to Bahrain* (8th edition). London: The Augustan Press.

Bibby, G. 1986. The origins of the Dilmun Civilization. In Shaikha Haya Ali Al Khalifa and M. Rice (eds.), *Bahrain through the ages: the Archaeology*. London: Kegan Paul International, pp. 108-116.

--. 1996. *Looking for Dilmun* (2nd edition). London: Stacey International.

Breuil, J-Y. 1999. The World's Largest Prehistoric Cemetery. In *Bahrain The Civilisation of the Two Seas. From Dilmun to Tylos* (exhibition catalogue). Paris: Institut du Monde, pp. 49-55.

Crawford, H. 2001. *Early Dilmun Seals from Saar*. London-Bahrain Archaeological Expedition,

Saar Excavation Report 2. Ludlow: Archaeology International Ltd.

Crawford, H., Killick, R. and Moon, J. 1997. *The Dilmun Temple at Saar*. London-Bahrain Archaeological Expedition, Saar Excavation Report 1. London: Kegan Paul International.

Dalongville, R. 1999. Bahrain, the Gulf's Natural Exception. In *Bahrain The Civilisation of the Two Seas. From Dilmun to Tylos* (exhibition catalogue). Paris: Institut du Monde, pp. 28-36.

Durand, Capt. E.L. 1879. *Report on the Antiquities of Bahrein*. Ms. on file, India Office Library, London.

--. 1880. Extracts from Report on the Islands and Antiquities of Bahrein (With Notes by Major-General H.C. Rawlinson). *Journal of the Royal Asiatic Society* 12: 189-227.

Frifelt, K. 2001. *Islamic Remains in Bahrain*. Moesgaard: Jutland Archaeological society.

Frohlich, B. 1982. A Preliminary Report on the Human Remains from Bahrain Island. In M. Ibrahim, *Excavations of the Arab Expedition at Sar el-Jisr, Bahrain.* Bahrain: Ministry of Information, pp. 91-98.

Glob, P.V. 1968. *Al-Bahrain. De danske ekspeditioner til oldtidens Dilmun*. Copenhagen: Gyldendal.

Højlund, F. 1999. Qal'at al-Bahrain in the Bronze Age. In *Bahrain The Civilisation of the Two Seas. From Dilmun to Tylos* (exhibition catalogue). Paris: Institut du Monde, pp. 73-76.

--. 2008. *The Burial Mounds of Bahrain*. Moesgaard: Jutland Archaeological Society.

Insoll, T. 2005. *The Land of Enki in the Islamic Era*. London: Kegan Paul.

Kervran, M. 1982. Preliminary Report on the Excavation of Qala'at al-Bahrain. In M. Kervran, A. Negre and M. Pirazzoli-t'Sertsevens, *Excavations of Qala'at al-Bahrain. 1st part (1977-1979)*. Bahrain: The Ministry of Information Directorate of Archaeology and Museums, pp. 59-84.

--. 1988. *Bahrain in the 16th century. An impregnable island*. Bahrain: Ministry of Information.

--. 1990. La Mosquée Al-Khamis à Bahrain: Son Histoire et ses Inscriptions. *Archéologie Islamique* 1: 7-23.

Killick, R. 1999. The Dilmun Temple at Saar. In *Bahrain The Civilisation of the Two Seas. From Dilmun to Tylos* (exhibition catalogue). Paris: Institut du Monde, pp. 107-114.

Killick, R. and Moon, J. 2005. *The Early Dilmun Settlement at Saar*. London-Bahrain Archaeological Expedition, Saar Excavation Report 3. Ludlow: Archaeology International Ltd.

Laursen, S. in press. Reconstructing the world's largest mound cemetery and its "living" population. Air-photographic survey of the burial mounds of Bahrain with estimates of the average size of the population in Early Dilmun, c. 2250-1800 BC. In P. Lombard and K. Al-Sindi, (eds.), *Proceedings of the Conference: "20 Years of Bahrain Archaeology, 1986-2006"*. Manama: Bahrain National Museum.

--. 2008. Early Dilmun and its rulers: new evidence of the burial mounds of the elite and the development of social complexity c. 2200-1750 BC. *Arabian Archaeology and Epigraphy* 19: 155-166.

Lewcock, R. 1986. The Traditional Architecture of Bahrain. In S.H. Al-Khalifa and M. Rice (eds.), *Bahrain Through the Ages. The Archaeology*. London: Kegan Paul International, pp. 485-96.

Miles, S.B. 1919 (1966). *The Countries and Tribes of the Persian Gulf*. London: Frank Cass.

Negre, A. 1982. Coins found at Qal'at al-Bahrain. In M. Kervran, A. Negre and M. Pirazzoli-t'Sertsevens, *Excavations of Qala'at al-Bahrain. 1st part (1977-1979)*. Bahrain: The Ministry of Information Directorate of Archaeology and Museums, pp. 85-94.

Nesbitt, M. 1993. Archaeobotanical evidence for early Dilmun diet at Saar, Bahrain. *Arabian archaeology and epigraphy* 4: 20-47.

Pirazzoli-t'Sertsevens, M. 1982. The Chinese Ceramics. In M. Kervran, A. Negre and M. Pirazzoli-t'Sertsevens, *Excavations of Qala'at al-Bahrain. 1st part (1977-1979)*. Bahrain: The Ministry of Information Directorate of Archaeology and Museums, pp. 95-104.

Rice, M. (ed.). 1984. Dilmun Discovered. The Early Years of Archaeology in Bahrain. London: Longman (on behalf of the Department of Antiquities and Museums, State of Bahrain.)

--. 1986. 'The island on the edge of the world'. In Shaikha Haya Ali Al Khalifa and M. Rice (eds.), *Bahrain through the ages: the Archaeology*. London: Kegan Paul International, pp. 116-124.

--. n.d. *The Temple Complex at Barbar, Bahrain. A Description and Guide*. Manama: Ministry for Information.

Smith, I. 2005. The mammal, bird, reptile, and mollusc remains from Bilad al-Qadim. In T. Insoll (ed.), *The Land of Enki in the Islamic Era*. London: Kegan Paul, pp. 193-232.

Uerpmann, M. and Uerpmann, H-P. 2005. Animal bone finds and their relevance to the ecology and economy of Saar. In R. Killick and J. Moon, *The*

Early Dilmun Settlement at Saar. London-Bahrain Archaeological Expedition, Saar Excavation Report 3. Ludlow: Archaeology International Ltd., pp. 293-308.

Vine, P. 1993. *Bahrain National Museum.* London: Immel Publishing Ltd.

Index

H

I

J

K

L